history at source

THE COLD WAR

E G Rayner

Hodder & Stoughton

A MEMBER OF THE HODDER HEADLINE GROUP

ACKNOWLEDGEMENTS

The cover illustration is a cartoon by John Jensen published in *Czechoslovakia: the Death of a Dream* in August 1968.

The publishers wish to thank the following for their permission to reproduce copyright illustrations:

John Jensen: cover; Popperfoto: p 48, p 49; Punch Publications p 55, p 93, p 94; Leslie Illingworth, Daily Mail/Solo Syndication and Literary Agency: p 92; Vicky, New Statesman/Centre for the Study of Cartoon and Caricature, University of Kent at Canterbury: p 95 top; © 1992 by Tribune Media Services; reprinted by permission of Editors Press Service, Inc: p 95 lower.

The Publishers would like to thank the following for permission to reproduce material in this volume:

Allen Unwin, now Unwin Hyman, an imprint of HarperCollins Publishers Ltd for the extract from *The Cold War and its Origins*, D F Fleming; Blackwell for the extract from *Khrushchev*, Roy Medvedev; André Deutsch Limited for the extracts from *Khrushchev Remembers*, N S Khrushchev (1971); BBC Enterprises Limited for the extract from *The Unsettled Peace*, Roger Morgan (1974); Chambers for the extract from *Politics in the Soviet Union* (1st edition), Ian Derbyshire pp 65–66 (1987); Random Century Group for the extract from *The Cold War As History*, Louis J Halle, Chatto & Windus; Longman Group UK for *A Contemporary Report on the Building of the Wall* from Keesings Contemporary Archives report of 23rd August 1961, *The Cold War from Soviet Reactions to the Chinese Invasion of North Vietnam 1979* as reported in Keesings Contemporary Archives October 1979, *The Cold War* from News Report in Keesings Contemporary Archives for November 1990; Oxford University Press for the Royal Institute of International Affairs, London for the extract *Survey of the Sino-Soviet Dispute*, Gittings, 1963–67 and *The Study of International Affairs*, Morgan; Princeton University Press for the extract *Lyndon Johnson and Vietnam*, Herbert V Schandler from *The Unmaking of a President* (1977); Times Newspapers Ltd 1989/91 for the extracts *The Russian Tricolour Flies Again* (23/8/91), *The Breaching of the Berlin Wall* (23/12/89) and *The Process of Change in the Soviet Union* (14/8/91); United Nations for the extract from *General Assembly Document, A/3592*; Weidenfeld & Nicolson for the extract from *The Politics of War*, G Kolko (1969)

Every effort has been made to trace and acknowledge ownership of copyright. The publishers will be glad to make suitable arrangements with any copyright holders whom it has not been possible to contact.

British Library Cataloguing in Publication Data
Rayner, E.G.
   The Cold War. – (History at source)
   I. Title   II. Series
   327.109

   ISBN 0–340–56545–4

First published 1992
Impression number   9
Year   2005 2004 2003 2002

Typeset by Wearset, Boldon Tyne and Wear
Printed in Great Britain for Hodder & Stoughton Educational, a division of Hodder Headline plc, 338 Euston Road, London, NW1 3BH by The Bath Press, Bath.

CONTENTS

PREFACE

Since the extension of modern history syllabuses into the period after 1945 there has been a steadily growing interest in the phenomenon commonly known as the 'Cold War', marking a clearly defined phase in the relations between the major powers after the Second World War. Many books have been written on this subject, and it has become a popular topic with students studying at A Level, AS Level, Higher Grade and beyond. At the same time, changes in the requirements of examination boards, particularly the introduction of source-based ('common core') questions, coursework and personal assignments, have increased the demands made on students and teachers alike.

This book is intended for those who are interested in the main phases of the Cold War from 1945 to the present date. It is hoped that it will provide a practical complement to existing textbooks and more specialized texts. The book concentrates on a number of central phases in the Cold War – origins, confrontation and *détente* – and introduces topics through collections of primary and secondary sources, concluding each with the type of questions likely to be encountered in examinations involving the use of sources. Practical advice is offered on the way to approach such questions, and a specimen answer is included. Guidance is also given on the approach to essay questions. Sample essay questions are provided with suggestions for relevant treatment; and again a specimen answer is included. Finally, a bibliography is given in order to help students and teachers with the use of available books.

It is hoped that this collection will prove useful for students working as part of an organized course or studying on their own without the help of a teacher.

APPROACHING SOURCE-BASED QUESTIONS

Source-based questions have become an important part of history examinations at all levels in recent years. Students who have studied History at GCSE or Standard Grade will have some experience of handling various types of sources. The questions based upon them are sometimes referred to as 'common core' questions because they aim to test historical skills irrespective of the factual content of the syllabus. Factual content is not what the 'common core' is about; this is exactly the difference between *stimulus-based* questions and *skills-based* questions. Some limited use of contextual questions, up to a total of 3 or 4 marks out of 25, is regarded as permissible as a means of 'getting into' the documents; but generally the questions call into play understanding, evaluation and interpretation. The skills students have already embarked upon at a lower level will continue to apply to a more advanced level, and the sources themselves will probably be more demanding.

During your studies you will have encountered both *primary* and *secondary* evidence. The distinction between the two is sometimes artificially exaggerated: all sources have their uses and limitations, and it is possible to worry unnecessarily about a 'hierarchy of sources'. The important thing for the student is to feel confident in understanding and handling all sources. The majority of sources in this book are primary sources, since they are the raw material from which historians work; and they are mostly taken from various kinds of documents, since this is the type most commonly found in examinations. However, the guidance given below will apply to *all* types of evidence, and there are some examples of secondary and non-documentary evidence included.

When students are faced with a piece of historical evidence there are certain questions that they should always ask of that source; but in examinations students will be asked specific questions set by an examiner, and in the light of the pressures of examinations – not the least of which is time – it is important to tackle these questions in an organized fashion. What follows is advice to be borne in mind when tackling examination questions of the source-based type.

It should be noted that different boards operate different length limits for documentary evidence in order that candidates shall not be confronted by too much reading. In practice the number of documents used is limited, since the passages otherwise would be too short to be of much value, and would leave candidates too little room

1

to search for internal evidence deriving from vocabulary or style. Boards also operate different devices of editing in order to make extracts easier to use. Some number lines sequentially so that candidates can refer to a passage without having to copy it out; others employ italic or underlining to give prominence to passages referred to in the sub-questions. Some boards give their documentary questions a *title* so that candidates do not have to spend a long time on the texts deciding whether to attempt the question or not; this title, and the *stem* of the question, i.e. the introductory sentence setting out the requirements of the question, should be studied before you embark upon it.

Answering documentary questions:

1 Skim through the documents quickly, making sure you have read all of them and that there are no others over the page. When you have done this, and decided that this is a question which you may attempt, read through the documents again, this time more carefully and slowly, taking in the overall meaning of each.

2 Pay particular attention to the *attribution* of each source, noting its author, date and place of origin. Note whether it is a document contemporary with the events or persons dealt with, or whether it is written later and with the benefit of hindsight. Note also the context in which it is produced, i.e. whether it is confidential or in the public domain, whether the author is an expert in the matter or merely an onlooker, and whether the recipient (if any) stands in a special relationship with the author or is otherwise privileged. Note, too, whether the document is in the original language or is translated.

3 Read through all the sub-questions (or 'items') attached to the documents. Before you embark on a question, remember that the opening items may be deceptively simple, but that the question may turn out to be too difficult in the later stages. Do not attempt to answer a question until you are satisfied that you can produce reasonable answers to all the items in it.

4 Look closely at the tariff of marks on offer, and tailor the length of your answer accordingly. There is no point in writing a lengthy paragraph to score 1 mark; a short sentence, a phrase, or even a single word may be enough. Nor can you expect to win 4 or 5 marks if you write no more than a few words on a more heavily weighted item. Unnecessarily long answers should be avoided, and above all you ought to avoid paraphrasing or copying out the document; but at the same time you should take care to provide enough 'meat' in your answer to warrant the award of the full tariff of marks.

5 Study the wording of the items closely. Some will ask you to use *only* your own knowledge in the answer; some will ask you to use *both* your knowledge *and* the sources; others will insist that you confine your answer to knowledge gleaned from the sources *alone*. You will lose marks if you ignore these instructions.

6 In writing your answers be sure to avoid irrelevant narrative. Use the document appropriately, using brief quotations from it if this serves to reinforce your answer. Do not introduce material not required for the purposes of the answer, or which is directly contrary to the sense of the document. If you are asked for a specific feature of the document, use the document for the answer; do not rely on what you imagine the document ought to say, but what it actually does.

7 If there are several sources to be consulted, ensure you make use of the ones to which you are directed. Candidates have been known to omit some, or even to choose the wrong ones.

8 Certain types of question require a particular type of response:
   a) Comparison of sources: be sure that you compare all the sources referred to in the item (see above).
   b) Commenting on the usefulness and limitations of sources: if asked to do both, be sure that you consider both aspects.
   c) Commenting on reliability: this is not the same as commenting on the usefulness of a source, though the two are sometimes confused.
   d) Responding to requests to 'analyse' or 'assess' the content of sources: do not be afraid to quote from the extract, but avoid too much direct paraphrasing. What is wanted is a considered judgement.
   e) Attempts at synthesis: a high-level skill which requires you to bring together several pieces of evidence and draw an overall conclusion.

9 Avoid spending too great a proportion of your time on the sources questions in examinations. Frequently candidates answer sources questions thoroughly but fail to allow themselves enough time for the rest of the examination paper. The proportion of time to be devoted to the sources questions should depend on the number of marks allocated to them in the paper.

10 If possible, read the published examiners' reports which will give you further indications as to the most useful approaches to adopt, and pitfalls to avoid.

Some useful vocabulary:

Authenticity	Is the document genuine, or is it a fraud?
Reliability	Is the document truthful, or is it misleading?
Validity	Is the document logically sound, or are the conclusions being drawn from its contents not supported by the evidence it provides?
Usefulness	Does the document cast important light on its subject, or is it only of peripheral importance?

Examples:

1 A report that President Gorbachev was shot in the Crimea in August 1991 whilst resisting arrest is not *authentic*, but is *false*.
2 An unsupported assertion that President Gorbachev encouraged the formation of a right-wing plot against himself in order to strengthen his political position in the Soviet Union is not *reliable*.
3 The implication that the attempted overthrow of President Gorbachev by Kremlin hard-liners materially strengthened his position with regard to the ambitions of Boris Yeltsin in the Russian Federation is not *valid*.
4 The admission that President Gorbachev never had time to clean his shoes during the whole time he was detained in the Crimea is not *important*.

A Note on this Collection of Sources

This collection intends to give some suggestions to teachers and realistic examples to students, either for use in schools and colleges or for purposes of self-study. However, the ideas put forward are meant to be flexible. If you wish, the questions or mark tariffs may be adapted, or entirely new questions devised; or the sources may be used as part of coursework or personal studies. You may even find it useful to collect together your own sources from the books recommended in the bibliography and draft your own appropriate questions.

1 THE SITUATION IN
POST-WAR GERMANY, 1945–46

In the closing years of the Second World War the Soviet Army
advanced over 1500 miles from Stalingrad into the heart of Germany,
and also overran much of the Balkans. Well aware of the draining
effect of the war on their military resources, and taking advantage of
groups of communists already in existence in the countries of central
and eastern Europe, Russian leaders began the task of establishing
regimes in those countries sympathetic to the Soviet Union, with a
view to creating a buffer zone between them and the combined forces
of the Western powers. For example in January 1945 Stalin
recognized the communist-dominated Lublin Committee as the
rightful government of Poland, and, in spite of promising at the Yalta
Conference in February to include in the new Polish government
representatives of Mikolajczyk's exiles in London, showed little
enthusiasm for these promises and continued to work towards a
purely communist regime for Poland.

The Western states regarded these governments as 'soviet satellites'
and began to insist on the holding of 'free and unfettered elections' in
the areas liberated at the end of the war. In the case of Poland the
Western powers continued to press the Russians at the time of the
Potsdam Conference in August 1945 to honour their pledge to give
some scope to non-communist elements in the new Polish
government, asking for free elections, universal suffrage and secret
ballots, and agreeing in return to a substantial extension of Polish
power westwards, as far as the line of the rivers Oder and Neisse.

Also at Potsdam, detailed arrangements were made for the division
of Germany into four zones of occupation, the three western zones
being apportioned to Britain, France and the United States and the
eastern zone being allotted to the Soviet Union. Berlin lay deep within
the Russian zone and special arrangements were made for the city,
which was itself divided into four sectors, reproducing in miniature
the partition of Germany as a whole. It was expected that a peace
settlement would follow which would deal with Germany as a whole.

But suspicions were not slow to grow. The West soon came to think,
in the words of Churchill, that 'the Russians are spreading across
Europe like a tide', and seized on Russian demands for German
forced labour and a large share in reparations as evidence of their bad
faith. Stalin, for his part, suspected the West of capitalist
expansionism and aggression, and could point to Truman's refusal to
share with him the secrets of the atom bomb as a pointer to British
and American duplicity. Each side blamed the other of breaking faith

over the Potsdam agreement to treat Germany as a single economic unit.

By 1946, the USA was beginning to press for the economic unification of the occupation zones of Germany as a preliminary measure towards the setting-up of an elected democratic government for the whole country. However, the Russians resisted these moves and continued to drain Germany of its industrial resources, even pressing for a share in reparations payments from the western zones. Western countries were not slow to ascribe the breakdown of occupation arrangements to the malevolence and expansionism of the Soviet Union. Shortly afterwards, the British and American zones of Germany were in fact unified, and the new arrangement was given the name 'Bizonia.'

Contemporary comments were virulent in the extreme, but, after the dust had settled, later commentators were able to take a more dispassionate view.

A Establishment of a Council of Foreign Ministers
I A 3 (i) The Council shall be authorized to draw up . . . treaties of peace with Italy, Romania, Bulgaria, Hungary and Finland and to propose settlements of territorial questions outstanding on the termination of the war in Europe. The Council shall be utilized for the preparation of a peace settlement for Germany to be accepted by the Government of Germany when a government . . . is established. . .

II A 2 So far as is practicable there shall be uniformity of treatment of the German population throughout Germany. . .

9 The administration in Germany should be directed towards the decentralization of the political structure and the development of local responsibility. To this end. . .
(ii) democratic political parties . . . shall be allowed. . .
(iii) representative and elective principles shall be introduced. . .
(iv) for the time being, no central German Government shall be established. . .

B 15 Allied controls shall be imposed upon the German economy but only to the extent necessary:
(a) to carry out programmes of industrial disarmament and . . . reparations
(b) to assure the production . . . of goods and services required to meet the needs of the occupying forces and displaced persons. . .

VIII Poland
A We have taken note with pleasure of the agreement reached among

representative Poles from Poland and abroad to make possible the formation, in accordance with the decisions reached at the Crimea Conference, of a Polish Government of National Unity recognized by the Three Powers. The establishment by the British and United States governments of diplomatic relations with the Polish Provisional Government has resulted in the withdrawal of their recognition from the former Polish Government in London, which no longer exists.

From the Protocol of Berlin (Potsdam Conference), 2 August 1945

B The 'Iron Curtain' Speech

A shadow has fallen upon the scenes so lately lighted by the Allied victory. Nobody knows what Soviet Russia and its Communist international organization intends to do in the immediate future, or what are the limits, if any, to their expansive and proselytizing tendencies. . . There is sympathy and goodwill in Britain . . . towards the peoples of all the Russias, and a resolve to persevere through many differences and rebuffs in establishing lasting friendships. . . It is my duty, however, to place before you certain facts about the present position in Europe.

From Stettin in the Baltic, to Trieste in the Adriatic, an iron curtain has descended across the continent. Behind that line lie all the capitals of the ancient states of Central and Eastern Europe – Warsaw, Berlin, Prague, Vienna, Budapest, Bucharest and Sofia. All these famous cities, and the populations around them, lie in the Soviet sphere, and all are subject in one form or another not only to Soviet influence, but to a high and increasing measure of control from Moscow. Athens alone, with its immortal glories, is free to decide its future in an election under British, American and French observation. The Russian-dominated Polish Government has been encouraged to make enormous and wrongful inroads upon Germany, and mass expulsions of millions of Germans on a scale grievous and undreamed of are now taking place. The Communist parties, which were very small in all these Eastern states of Europe, have been raised to pre-eminence and power far beyond their numbers, and are seeking everywhere to obtain totalitarian control. Police governments are prevailing in nearly every case, and so far, except in Czechoslovakia, there is no true democracy. . . An attempt is being made by the Russians in Berlin to build up a quasi-Communist party in their zone of occupied Germany by showing special favours to groups of left-wing German leaders.

Speech of Winston Churchill at Fulton, Miss., USA, 5 March 1946

C US Comments on the Potsdam Agreement

It is not in the interests of the German people or in the interests of world

7

peace that Germany should become a pawn . . . in a military struggle for power between East and West. . .

The United States is prepared to carry out fully the principles outlined in the Potsdam Agreement on demilitarization and reparations.

The carrying out of the Potsdam Agreement has, however, been obstructed by the failure of the Allied Control Council to take the necessary steps to enable the German economy to function as an economic unit. . .

The equitable distribution of essential commodities between the several zones . . . has not been arranged, although that too is expressly required by the Potsdam Agreement. . .

The working out of a balanced economy throughout Germany . . . has not been accomplished, although that too is expressly required by the Potsdam Agreement. . .

The United States is firmly of the belief that Germany should be administered as an economic unit and that zonal barriers should be completely obliterated. . .

The American Government . . . has formally announced that it is its intention to unify the economy of its own zone with any or all of the other zones willing to participate in the unification. . .

The Potsdam Agreement . . . was not intended to prevent progress towards a central government . . . but it was intended to prevent the establishment of a strong central government dominating the German people instead of being responsible to their democratic will.

Speech of James Byrnes, US Secretary of State, Stuttgart, Germany,
6 September 1946

D Soviet Policies in Post-war Europe

More aware than anyone else of their own weaknesses in the event of a conflict with the United States, the Russians pursued a conservative and cautious line wherever they could find local non-Communist groups willing to abjure the traditional diplomacy of the *cordon sanitaire** and anti-Bolshevism. . . They showed neither more nor less respect for an unborn functional democracy in Eastern Europe than the Americans and British evidenced in Italy, Greece or Belgium. For neither the Americans, British nor Russians were willing to permit democracy to run its course anywhere in Europe at the cost of damaging their vital strategic and economic interests. . . The Russians had no intention of Bolshevizing Eastern Europe in 1945 if . . . they could find alternatives.

From G. Kolko, *The Politics of War* (1969)

* *cordon sanitaire* = a barrier isolating a state considered to be dangerous

E Allied Differences in Post-war Europe
The condominium of the 'Big Three' was toppling even before it had taken solid shape. It would be futile to try to establish which of the Allies made the first decisive move away from it. Through the labyrinth of conflicting versions and recriminations it is hardly possible to trace the first 'broken pledge.' The pledges of the Allies had, anyhow, been so vague and contained so many loopholes that by reference to the text each side could justify its conduct. The point is that the fundamental cleavage between the Allies could not but lead the one side, or the other, or both, to abandon mutual commitments. In this *mariage de convenance** the thought of the inevitability of divorce had been in the back of the mind of each partner from the beginning; and almost from the beginning each side had to think about the advantages it would secure and the disadvantages from which it would suffer at the moment of the divorce.

From Isaac Deutscher, *Stalin* (1969)

* *mariage de convenance* = a marriage for reasons of material advantage, and not for love.

Questions

1 Using your own knowledge, explain the events directly leading to the signing of the Protocol from which Source A is taken. **(3 marks)**

2 Using Source B and your own knowledge, explain Winston Churchill's increasing dissatisfaction with the situation in central and eastern Europe in March 1946. **(3 marks)**

3 With reference to Source C, explain the reasons why the United States concluded in September 1946 that the Soviet Union was violating the terms agreed in Source A. **(4 marks)**

4 In what ways does the explanation given in Source D of Soviet policies in Europe, 1945–46, differ from those offered in Sources B and C? **(6 marks)**

5 To what extent do Sources D and E offer more impartial explanations of allied policies in post-war Europe than Sources B and C? What evidence of hindsight do Sources D and E contain? **(6 marks)**

6 Which of the five Sources A–E in your opinion is the most reliable? How far do all the sources enable the historian to construct an accurate picture of events in Europe, 1945–46? **(8 marks)**

2 THE ATOMIC BOMB

In the mid-summer of 1945 the US government decided to use an atomic device against the mainland of Japan. There seem to have been three chief reasons for this decision: 1) to save the American lives which would be lost during a lengthy and expensive campaign in the Pacific, 2) to shorten the war, and 3) to forestall Soviet intervention in the war and so restrict Russia's influence in the Far East. All these motives have been seriously questioned since the decision was taken, but at the time Truman's attitude fell only a little short of elation: 'If the bomb explodes, as I think it will, I'll . . . have a hammer on those boys!' [the Russians].

In early August, two A-bombs were dropped, the first on Hiroshima on Honshu and the second a few days later on Nagasaki on Kyushu, both with devastating results. Only a few days later the Japanese government offered to capitulate. Preliminary terms were agreed and the final unconditional surrender ceremony took place aboard the US battleship *Missouri* in Tokyo Bay on 2 September.

At Potsdam in July, the American President had deliberately concealed from the Russians the existence of the A-bomb, with vague talk about 'a new weapon that had been developed.' Truman seems to have hoped that the news of the first use of the weapon would make the Russians apprehensive and thus more amenable to US wishes in Europe; but in fact Stalin, either through ignorance of the bomb's true potential or through a more far-sighted realization that the US President would never dare to use it against them, refused to allow himself to be intimidated. He was however sufficiently sure of the bomb's potential to give urgent priority to the production of a Soviet bomb and to embark on industrial research in order to explore the other uses of atomic energy. The Soviet Union produced its own A-bomb as early as 1949; by 1953 both the USA and the USSR were equipped with H-bombs. By this time cold war attitudes had hardened into deep mutual mistrust.

A Churchill on the Atomic Bomb

The bomb brought peace, but men alone can keep that peace, and henceforward they will keep it under penalties which threaten the survival, not only of civilization, but of humanity itself. I may say that I am in entire agreement with the President that the secrets of the atomic bomb shall so far as possible not be imparted at the present time to any other country in the world. This is in no design or wish for arbitrary power but for the common safety of the world. . .

The United States stand at this moment at the summit of the world. I rejoice that this should be so. Let them act up to the level of their power and their responsibility, not for themselves but for others, for all men in all lands, and then a brighter day may dawn upon human history. So far as we know, there are at least three and perhaps four years before the concrete progress made in the United States can be overtaken. In these three years we must remould the relationships of all men, wherever they dwell, in all the nations. We must remould them in such a way that these men do not wish or dare to fall upon each other for the sake of vulgar and outdated ambitions or for passionate differences in ideology, and that international bodies of supreme authority may give peace on earth and decree justice among men.

Winston Churchill, in a speech to the House of Commons, 17 August 1945

B The Soviet Attitude towards the Development of Nuclear Energy
It is not possible at present for a technical secret of any great size to remain the exclusive possession of some one country or some narrow circle of countries.

This being so, the discovery of atomic energy should not encourage either a propensity to exploit the discovery in the play of forces in international policy or an attitude of complacency as regards the future of the peace-loving nations. . .

In our days of advanced technology . . . attention in economic planning must be focused on problems of technology, on the problem of raising the technological power of our industry and training highly-skilled technological trainers. We must keep level with the achievements of present-day world technology in all branches of industry and economic life, and provide conditions for the utmost advance of Soviet science and technology.

The enemy interrupted our peaceful creative endeavour. But we shall make up properly for all lost time and see to it that our country shall flourish. We will have atomic energy and many other things, too.

V.M. Molotov in an address on the 28th Anniversary of the Russian Revolution, 6 November 1945

C Public Comments in the Soviet Union on the Atomic Bomb
The atomic bomb is a signal for reactionaries all over the world to agitate for a new crusade against the Soviet Union. . .

It is unthinkable in our country to have a situation such as exists in foreign countries where official representatives sing hymns of praise to international co-operation while influential newspapers and magazines openly make appeals for war.

Article in the Moscow *New Times*, 18 November 1945

D The USA in the Role of World Policeman

With the strategic location of airfields from the Philippines to Alaska, on the coast of Asia, from Alaska to the Azores in the South Atlantic [*sic*], we can drop, at a moment's notice, atomic bombs on any spot on the world's surface and return to our base. . . With vision and guts and plenty of atomic bombs, ultra-modern planes and strategically-located airbases the United States can outlaw wars of aggression. . .

The world organization which I am thinking of is one designed to stop war with the atomic bomb in the hands of the United States as the club behind the door, to be used only when a bandit nation goes berserk.

Senator Edwin Johnson in a speech to the US Senate, 28 November 1945

E An American Journalist's View of the Atomic Bomb

No atomic bombardment could destroy the Red Army; it could destroy only the industrial means of supplying it. The Russian defence to atomic attack is, therefore, self-evident; it is to overrun continental Europe with infantry, and defy us to drop atomic bombs on Poland, Cezchoslovakia, Austria. . . The more we threaten to demolish Russian cities, the more obvious it is that the Russian defence would be to ensconce themselves in European cities which we could not demolish without massacring hundreds of thousands of our own friends.

Walter Lippmann, writing in the *Nashville Tennessean*, 15 March 1946

F Mao Zedong on the Atomic Bomb

The Soviet Union is a defender of world peace and a powerful factor preventing the domination of the world by US reactionaries. Because of the existence of the Soviet Union, it is absolutely impossible for the reactionaries in the United States and the world to realize their ambitions. That is why the US reactionaries rabidly hate the Soviet Union and actually dream of destroying this socialist state. . .

The atom bomb is a paper tiger which the US reactionaries use to scare people. It looks terrible, but in fact it isn't. Of course, the atom bomb is a weapon of mass slaughter, but the outcome of a war is decided by the people, not by one or two new types of weapon.

All reactionaries are paper tigers. In appearance, reactionaries are terrifying, but in reality they are not so powerful. From the long-term point of view, it is not the reactionaries but the people who are really powerful.

Mao Zedong, in a newspaper interview with Anna Louisa Strong, August 1946

Questions

1 Why, according to Source A, does Churchill 'rejoice' that in mid-1945 the United States stood 'at the summit of the world'? **(3 marks)**

2 Using Sources B and C and your own knowledge, explain Soviet official and popular reactions to the possession by the Western allies of the atomic weapon. **(6 marks)**

3 Using only Sources D and E, show how and why attitudes within the United States differed over the use of the atomic bomb. **(6 marks)**

4 Using Source F and your own knowledge, explain the importance of Mao Zedong's comments on the atomic bomb in August 1946. **(6 marks)**

5 How far do Sources A–F help to explain the controversies between the Western powers and the communists over the importance of the nuclear developments of 1945–46? **(9 marks)**

3 THE TRUMAN DOCTRINE AND THE MARSHALL PLAN, 1947

The ending of the Second World War saw the extension of Soviet influence in eastern Europe and in the Balkans. The Soviet Union saw this as a protective manoeuvre against the massive military might of the Western allies, but both Churchill and President Truman suspected a deep-laid communist plot to take over smaller countries weakened by the war and to transform them into obedient 'satellites'. For whatever motive, the USSR steadily extended its power. Soon Russian pressure on Greece, Turkey and Iran aroused great alarm in the West. Traditionally, Britain had been strongly entrenched in this area, but British decline, accelerated by the war, obliged the United States to assume responsibility for its defence. In March 1947 the US President set out his policy for the defence of the area against communism in a speech to the Houses of the American Congress, a policy known as the Truman Doctrine. This policy subsidized the governments of Greece and Turkey with grants of about $400m, strengthening the pro-Western governments of both those countries.

By the spring of 1947 it had also become clear that the desperately-needed economic recovery of Europe was not taking place. Devastation was widespread through much of the continent, food and raw materials were short, production was lagging, and the problems brought about by refugees and displaced persons were as great as ever. The American answer was the Marshall Plan, introduced in an address by the US Secretary of State at Harvard University in June 1947. The Plan was devised as a programme of economic stabilization conceived in the interests of the recipients as well as the givers. Though it was made available to the powers of eastern Europe, and though some of them, like Poland and Czechoslovakia, would dearly have liked to avail themselves of it, the Soviet Union was deeply suspicious not only of the slight implied, but of the possibility of the strings that might have been attached to it, with the result that the communist states were persuaded not to ask for support. Altogether some $12,500m were spent on western European countries over the next three years. The Europeans, at a conference of 16 nations, produced their European Recovery Programme (ERP) to plan its use in July 1947, and this led to the establishment in April 1948 of the Organization for European Economic Co-operation (OEEC). This lasted throughout the 1950s, and at the end of 1960 was given a further lease of life in the form of the Organization for Economic Co-operation and Development (OECD).

There was mistrust between East and West over the Truman

Doctrine and the Marshall Plan. In the West, the Americans made great play with their magnanimity whilst being relieved that they did not have to shoulder the burdens of inefficient communist economies; in the East, communist leaders congratulated themselves on keeping out of the clutches of the capitalist world, but were forced to tighten their belts and soldier on without much-needed support.

A President Truman on the Soviet Threat in Post-war Europe

There isn't a doubt in my mind that Russia intends an invasion of Turkey and the seizure of the Black Sea Straits on the Mediterranean. Unless Russia is faced with an iron fist and strong language another war is in the making. Only one language do they understand: 'How many divisions have you?' . . . We should maintain complete control over Japan and the Pacific. We should rehabilitate China and create a strong central government there. We should do the same for Korea. Then we should insist on the return of our ships from Russia and force a settlement of the Lend-Lease debt of Russia. I'm tired of babying the Soviets.

President Truman, in a letter to Secretary of State James Byrnes,
5 January 1946

B The US President Announces the Truman Doctrine

At the present moment in world history nearly every nation must choose between alternative ways of life. The choice is too often not a free one.

One way of life is based upon the will of the majority, and is distinguished by free institutions, representative government, free elections, guarantees of individual liberty, freedom of speech and religion and freedom from political oppression.

The second way of life is based upon the will of a minority forcibly imposed upon the majority. It relies upon terror and oppression, a controlled press and radio, fixed* elections and the suppression of personal freedom.

I believe that it must be the policy of the United States to support peoples who are resisting attempted subjugation by armed minorities or by outside pressures.

I believe that we must assist free peoples to work out their own destiny in their own way.

President Truman, in an Address to the US Congress, 12 March 1947

* fixed (US) = stage-managed, contrived.

C Soviet Comments on the Truman Doctrine

Whatever pretexts are used to vindicate American claims to domination in Greece, they cannot be justified by a defence of the freedom and independence of the Greek people. American arguments for rendering assistance to Turkey are based upon a threat to the integrity of Turkish territory, though nothing threatens Turkish integrity. . . What is such monopolistic 'American responsibility' but a smokescreen for a plan of expansion? Justifications to the effect that the USA is called upon to 'save' Greece and Turkey from expansion on the part of so-called 'totalitarian' states are not new. Hitler also referred to the Bolsheviks when he wanted to open the road to conquests for himself. Now they try to take Greece and Turkey under their control and by raising a clamour about 'totalitarianism' attempt to disguise their plans of expansion.

Leading article in *Izvestia*, 17 March 1947

D Secretary of State Marshall Announces his Plan

Europe's requirements for the next three or four years of foreign food and other essential products – principally from America – are so much greater than her present ability to pay that she must have substantial additional help, or face economic, social and political deterioration of a very grave character. . .

It is logical that the United States should do whatever it is able to do to assist in the return of normal economic health to the world, without which there can be no political stability and no assured peace.

Our policy is directed not against any country or doctrine, but against hunger, poverty, desperation and chaos. Its purpose should be the revival of a working economy in the world so as to permit the emergence of political and social conditions in which free institutions can exist. Such assistance, I am convinced, must not be on a piecemeal basis as various crises develop. Any assistance that this government may develop in the future should provide a cure rather than a mere palliative.

Secretary of State George Marshall, in an address at Harvard University, 5 June 1947

E Soviet Comments on the Marshall Plan

(i) [The Truman Doctrine and the Marshall Plan] are both an embodiment of the American design to enslave Europe. [The United States has] launched an attack on the principle of national sovereignty. By contrast, the Soviet Union indefatigably upholds the principle of real equality and protection of the sovereign rights of all nations, large and small. . . The Soviet Union will bend every effort in order that [the

Marshall Plan] be doomed to failure. . . The Communist parties of France, Italy, Great Britain and other countries . . . must take up the standard in defence of the national independence and sovereignty of their countries.

A.A. Zhdanov, at the refounding conference of the Cominform in Polish Silesia, 22 September 1947

(ii) The ruling clique of American imperialists . . . has taken the path of outright expansion, of enslaving the weakened capitalist states of Europe and the colonial and dependent countries. It has chosen the path of hatching new war plans against the Soviet Union and the new democracies. . . The clearest and most specific expression of the policy . . . is provided by the Truman-Marshall plans. [With regard to] such countries as Yugoslavia and Poland, the United States and Great Britain are pursuing a terrorist policy. . . Imitating the Hitlerites, the new aggressors are using blackmail and extortion.

G.M. Malenkov, at the same conference

Questions

1 Using Sources A and B, and your own knowledge, describe the circumstances in which the Truman Doctrine was introduced in 1947.   **(4 marks)**

2 Use Sources A and B to analyse the differences between Truman's private and public utterances about the Soviet threat.   **(4 marks)**

3 What similarities may be detected in the terms in which the Truman Doctrine (Source B) and the Marshall Plan (Source D) were announced in 1947? Does the evidence of these two sources bear out the opinion commonly held at the time that the two were different facets of the same policy?   **(8 marks)**

4 Use the two extracts quoted in Source E, and your own knowledge, to explain the purposes for which the Cominform was refounded in 1947.   **(6 marks)**

5 To what extent do all the Sources A–E show that the conflict between the Western and the Eastern powers in 1947 was not so much a financial and economic struggle as an ideological one?   **(8 marks)**

4 THE CRISIS OVER BERLIN, 1948–49

From the beginning of 1947 the American and British occupation zones of Germany merged to form one economic unit, often known as Bizonia. In this area, Germans were increasingly encouraged to play a part, and were offered membership of the Economic Council there from its foundation in May 1947. ERP was soon extended to Germany as well as the other Western European states. By 1948 German nationals were participating in local and regional government, and were assuming financial and economic responsibilities, though it was American dollar aid that chiefly sustained the recovery. The Soviet Union registered repeated protests, but nevertheless the Western zones, which by now included the French, adopted a new currency in order to re-establish financial stability.

On the eve of the currency reform, inflation, shortages and demoralization had largely destroyed the value of the old money. A single cigarette cost 25 marks, a pound of coffee 1500 marks. The income of workers varied between 300 and 400 marks per month. On 20 June a new currency, the Deutsche Mark, was introduced into the Western zones, replacing the old Reichsmark which was no longer valid. Savings and bank holdings were reduced; every 100 Reichsmarks were now worth 6.5 of the new Deutsche Marks.

The Russians denounced this as a violation of the terms of the Potsdam Agreement, and three days later, also disregarding it, retaliated by announcing a currency reform of their own for the Soviet Zone and for Berlin. The Western allies were unwilling to allow a new currency, over which they had no control, to circulate in their part of Berlin, and as a result introduced their own Deutsche Mark into the city also. The next day the Russians cut off all communications by road, rail and canal between West Germany and West Berlin. So began a blockade of the city which lasted for the next 11 months. Only the Berlin Air Lift, a round-the-clock mission to ferry foodstuffs and materials into Berlin by air, prevented the city from being starved into submission by the Soviet armies.

In May 1949 Stalin, who had throughout drawn back from attacking the incoming planes, conceded defeat by raising the blockade. But the Western powers had already signed the North Atlantic Treaty, which came into effect in September, when NATO was set up for the defence of the whole strategic area. Constitutional discussions had already been taking place on the future political shape of West Germany, and the German Federal Republic came into being on 23 May, shortly after the raising of the Berlin Blockade.

West Germany achieved complete independence in 1955, when it was also accepted into membership of NATO.

The West saw the whole episode as a victory over Soviet expansionism, the Soviet leadership as a somewhat desperate effort to delay the emergence of a powerful and western-oriented Germany and to bolster up an already crumbling Eastern bloc. Germany itself paid the price; it remained divided until 1989.

A Economic Reform in Western Germany

The continuous failure of the Council of Foreign Ministers to reach quadripartite agreement has created a situation in Germany which, if permitted to continue, would have increasingly unfortunate consequences for Western Europe. It was, therefore, necessary that urgent political and economic problems arising out of this situation in Germany should be solved. . .

Discussions took place among the US, UK and French delegations on certain limited aspects of the question of reparations from Germany relating to internal policy in the zones for which they are responsible. . .

It was agreed that for the political and economic well-being of the countries of Western Europe and of a democratic Germany there must be a close association of their economic life. Since it has not proved possible to achieve economic unity in Germany, and since the Eastern zone has been prevented from playing its part in the ERP, the three Western powers have agreed that close co-operation should be established among themselves and among the occupation authorities in Western Germany in all matters arising out of the ERP. . .

It was agreed that a federal form of government, adequately protecting the rights of the respective states but at the same time providing for adequate central authority, is best adapted for the eventual re-establishment of German unity at present disrupted. Moreover, in order to facilitate the association of Western Germany with the ERP, the three delegations concerned further agreed that prompt action should be taken to co-ordinate as far as possible the economic policies of the three zones in such matters as foreign and inter-zonal trade, customs and freedom of movement for persons and goods.

Official communiqué after Three-Power Talks on Western Germany,
6 March 1948

B The Soviet Reaction to Western Currency Reform

[Western currency reform] is against the wishes and interests of the German people and in the interests of the American, British and French monopolists. . . The separate currency reform completes the splitting of

Germany. It is a breach of the Potsdam decisions and the control mechanism for Germany which envisaged the treatment of Germany as an economic whole. The Western powers are trying to excuse themselves by claiming that it was impossible to agree on a four-power currency reform for the whole of Germany. By this move they are simply trying to deceive public opinion. In the Control Council, the Soviet representatives took every possible opportunity of reaching agreement on common currency reform. It is clear that the Western representatives used the discussions in the Control Council as a cover, under cloak of which they prepared in secret for separate currency reform. The American, French and British monopolists in the Western zones are supported in their policy of splitting Germany by the big German capitalists and the *Junkers* who helped Fascism to power and prepared the Second World War. Separate currency reform strengthens the political and economic position of these reactionaries and harms the working people. The introduction of two currencies in Germany will mean that trade relations within the country will be destroyed. Inter-zonal trade will become in practice trade between two separate states, since two different currencies will be used. The prerequisites for free passenger traffic and goods traffic between the occupation zones will be destroyed.

Proclamation of Marshal Sokolovsky, Soviet Military Governor of Berlin,
18 June 1948

C The Achievements of the Berlin Air Lift

In the 318 days since the air lift began on 28 June 1948, British and US aircraft have made 195,530 flights to Berlin, carrying 1,583,686 short tons of food, coal and other stores, of which British aircraft have made 63,612 flights carrying 369,347 tons, and American aircraft 131,918 flights carrying 1,214,339 tons. The British total . . . was made up of approximately 185,000 tons of food, 97,000 tons of coal, 50,000 tons of fuel, 21,000 tons of miscellaneous cargoes, and 15,000 tons of supplies for the British services in Berlin. In the reverse direction, British aircraft carried out of Berlin about 30,000 tons of freight and over 65,000 passengers. Although the British contributing to the air lift, in number of flights and tonnage, was about one-quarter of the total, the RAF was responsible for the bulk of the ground organization (6 of the 8 dispatching airfields being in the British zone), and over 500,000 tons was flown into Gatow airfield (in the British sector of Berlin) alone. . . Gatow, which at present handles nearly 1,000 aircraft movements in 24 hours, can claim to be the busiest airfield in the world in that it averaged 540 movements a day over the whole period of the air lift.

Arthur Henderson, British Secretary for Air, 11 May 1949

D The End of the Air Lift

HM Government will approach the new meeting of the Council of
Foreign Ministers in the same spirit of firmness and reasonableness. I
am hopeful that the basis for an enduring settlement of the German
problem will be found at the forthcoming meeting. We shall not
abandon in that settlement the principles for which we have always
stood in regard to Germany. We have succeeded in standing firm in
Berlin because of the air lift. I have paid tribute to the air lift before, but
now more than ever it is right to say how much this country owes to the
skill and devotion of the crews and the ground staff, both British,
American and Commonwealth, who have taken part in this gigantic
operation. It will continue until the situation has been finally cleared up,
but I am sure that the House will agree that no praise and no thanks can
be too much for the men and women who have contributed to its
success.

Ernest Bevin, British Foreign Secretary, speaking to the House of Commons,
5 May 1949

E The North Atlantic Treaty, 1949

Preamble. The Parties to this Treaty reaffirm their faith in the purposes
and principles of the Charter of the United Nations, and their desire to
live in peace with all peoples and all governments.

They are determined to safeguard the freedom, common heritage
and civilization of their peoples, founded on the principles of
democracy, individual liberty and the rule of law.

They seek to promote stability and well-being in the North Atlantic
area.

They are resolved to unite their efforts for collective defence and for
the preservation of peace and security.

They therefore agree to this North Atlantic Treaty.

Article 1. The Parties undertake, as set forth in the Charter of the United
Nations, to settle any international disputes in which they may be
involved by peaceful means in such a manner that international peace
and security, and justice, are not endangered. . .

Article 2. They will seek to eliminate conflict in their international
economic policies and will encourage economic collaboration between
any or all of them. . .

Article 4. The Parties will consult together whenever, in the opinion of
any of them, the territorial integrity, political independence or security
of any of the Parties is threatened.

Article 5. The Parties agree that an armed attack against one or more of
them in Europe or North America shall be considered an attack against

them all; and consequently they agree that, if such an armed attack occurs, each of them, in exercise of the right of individual or collective self-defence recognized by Article 51 of the Charter of the United Nations, will assist the Party or Parties so attacked by taking forthwith . . . such action as it deems necessary, including the use of armed force, to restore and maintain the security of the North Atlantic area.

Any such armed attack and all measures taken as a result thereof shall immediately be reported to the Security Council. Such measures shall be terminated when the Security Council has taken the measures necessary to restore and maintain international peace and security. . .

Article 9. The Parties hereby establish a Council, on which each of them shall be represented, to consider matters concerning the implementation of this Treaty.

From the North Atlantic Treaty, 4 April 1949

Questions

1 How does Source A help to illustrate the concern felt by the Western Allies for the German question in 1948? **(4 marks)**

2 Estimate the reliability of Source B as historical evidence. **(4 marks)**

3 Granted the authenticity of Sources A and B, how valid are the explanations they put forward for responsibility for the crisis which occurred over Berlin in 1948–49? **(8 marks)**

4 Referring to Sources C and D, and to your own knowledge, indicate the importance of air power during the Berlin Blockade, June 1948–May 1949. **(6 marks)**

5 Use Source E to show how the conclusion of the treaty from which the source is taken bears out Bevin's determination in Source D that 'we shall not abandon in that settlement the principles for which we have always stood in regard to Germany.' **(8 marks)**

5 ORIGINS OF THE KOREAN WAR

The USSR declared war on Japan only a few days before the Japanese capitulation in 1945, but was in time to put Soviet forces into North Korea as the war came to an end. Like Germany, the country was then temporarily partitioned, the Russians occupying the area north of the 38th parallel, and the Americans the area south of it. South Korea was more populous than the North, and the Americans seem to have hoped, by establishing a democratic constitution in the South, that free elections would eventually enable their supporters to take over the whole country after the communist minority had been outvoted.

Civil war followed in China between the Nationalist forces of Jiang Jieshi (Chiang Kai-shek) and the Communists under Mao Zedong (Mao Tse-tung). In spite of the massive aid which the Americans had given to him over a period of years, Jiang did not have the ability or the spirit to win, and in 1949 fled from the mainland to take refuge on Taiwan, where he continued to masquerade as the rightful ruler of China. The idea took root in the USA, fostered by the anti-communist smear campaign of Senator Macarthy in Washington, that it was only irresolution and latent sympathy for communism in government circles (what he called 'un-American activities') that had lost this struggle against the forces of evil. Thus those who favoured an accommodation with international communism were frightened into silence, and a new note of toughness crept into US policy.

Meantime, by 1948 both the USSR and the USA withdrew their forces from Korea, leaving separate governments behind them whilst continuing to exercise an advisory role in their former zones. The National Assembly in Seoul, the Southern capital, left 100 seats vacant (out of 303) to be filled after unification by representatives from the North; but Kim Il-sung, the Northern leader, had no intention of taking up the offer. Kim and the tightly-knit communist clique which ruled North Korea continued to wrangle with Syngman Rhee and his authoritarian cronies in the South about the future of the country. There is evidence that each side sought to provoke the other into a false move whilst themselves making threatening noises against their rivals.

In June 1950 war broke out and a northern army of about 130,000 men poured into the South, capturing the Southern capital and pressing back the ineffectual Southern armies into a pocket round the southern port of Pusan.

Acting with exemplary swiftness, the Americans, invoking the aid of Britain and 14 other friendly countries, and clad in the authority of

23

the United Nations, came to the aid of the South. They were under the command of the US General MacArthur. Assisted by a sea-borne landing at Inchon, not far from Seoul, the troops of the anti-communist coalition swept northward in a well-armed offensive and by September 1950 had driven Kim's armies back to the 38th parallel. When they continued to advance, their objective became the liberation and unification of the whole peninsula.

A Secretary of State Dean Acheson's View of the Communist Victory in China, 1949

The reasons for the failures of the Chinese National Government appear in some detail in the attached record. They do not stem from any inadequacy of American aid. Our military observers on the spot have reported that the Nationalist armies did not lose a single battle during the crucial year of 1948 through lack of arms or ammunition. The fact was that the decay which our observers had detected in Chongqing (Chungking) early in the war had fatally sapped the powers of resistance of the Kuomintang. Its leaders had proved incapable of meeting the crisis confronting them, its troops had lost the will to fight, and its Government had lost popular support. The Communists, on the other hand, through a ruthless discipline and fanatical zeal, attempted to sell themselves as guardians and liberators of the people. The Nationalist armies did not have to be defeated; they disintegrated. History has proved again and again that a regime without faith in itself and an army without morale cannot survive the test of battle.

Dean Acheson, in Department of State records, US relations with China,
August 1950

B Chinese Communist Comment on Dean Acheson's Statement of US Policy in the Far East

The whole world knows that the US Government, in an attempt to annex China, has supported Jiang Jieshi in waging large-scale civil war, denying the Chinese people any opportunity to live in independence and peace. The US Government is supplying the Jiang Jieshi brigands with aircraft to bomb the mainland of China. It is employing similar methods in support of the puppets Bao Dai, Syngman Rhee and Quirino in undermining national independence movements in Vietnam, South Korea and the Philippines. Acheson says to the Chinese people: 'Why don't you ask for American aid?' But from their personal experience the Chinese people have realized what American so-called 'aid' means. It means death for millions; it means the loss of national freedom and rights. Since the Chinese rid themselves of American 'aid' things have gone well for China, and she has really become independent. . . These ridiculous threats are already anachronisms. The affairs of the Asian peoples will be settled by the Asian peoples themselves, and must never be interfered with by such American imperialists as Acheson and company on the other side of the Pacific.

> Zhou Enlai (Chou En-lai), Premier and Foreign Secretary of Communist China, in a statement to the Chinese News Agency, Beijing (Peking), 18 March 1950

C US Policy on Forestalling Communism in the Far East

[We advocate] an immediate and large-scale build-up in our military and general strength and that of our allies with the intention of righting the power balance and in the hope that through means other than all-out war we could induce a change in the nature of the socialist system. . .

The United States . . . can strike out on a bold and massive program of rebuilding the West's defensive potential to surpass that of the Soviet world, and of meeting each fresh challenge promptly and unequivocally. . . This means virtual abandonment by the United States of trying to distinguish between national and global security. It also means the end of subordinating security needs to the traditional budgeting restrictions; of asking 'How much security can we afford?' In other words, security must henceforth become the dominant element in the national budget, and other elements must be accommodated to it. . .

This new concept of the security needs of the nation calls for annual appropriations of the order of $50 billion*, or not much below the former wartime levels.

> Secret statement in National Security Council paper no. 68, State and Defence Department, Washington, April 1950

* Security appropriations when the document was produced amounted to $13 billion per annum.

D The Beginnings of the Korean War

The Russian military were as dubious of the North Koreans as many American military men were of the South Koreans. . . According to General Kalinov, members of the Soviet military mission wondered why in preparing a modern army for North Korea nothing was done to organize an air force. . .

General Zakharov explained . . . that it would have been easy to organize an air force of 1000 planes since there was no lack of pilots. There were nearly 500 Koreans who had served with the Red Army and as many other Korean pilots who had flown with the Chinese army. But, General Zakharov explained, 'It is necessary to be careful with these

Koreans. . . We are going to form a modern army . . . but we are not going to act like the sorcerer's apprentice, creating a force which could make mischief in the Far East.' The general said that the North Koreans, if given an air force, might sweep down to Pusan, bomb war vessels in the straits which separate Korea from Japan, and strike at Japan itself. 'This would bring war with the United States,' the Soviet General said, 'and we are not interested in provoking such a war.'

If the Russians were afraid that the North Koreans might embroil them with the United States, there were Americans no less concerned lest the South Koreans set the Far East aflame. In October 1949 . . . Syngman Rhee boasted in a public speech that the South could take Pyongyang, the Northern capital, in three days, and complained that he was stopped from doing so only by the United States which feared that such action might precipitate World War III. Rhee's Defence Minister, making a 'purely social call' on MacArthur on 31 October and 'not asking for more aid', told a press conference his troops were ready to drive into North Korea. 'If we had our own way,' he said, 'we should have started up already. . . We are strong enough to march up and take Pyongyang within a few days.'

From I.F. Stone, *The Hidden History of the Korean War*, (1952)

E US Reactions to the Outbreak of the Korean War

In Korea the Government forces, which were armed to prevent border raids and to preserve internal security, were attacked by invading forces from North Korea. The Security Council of the United Nations called upon the invading troops to cease hostilities and to withdraw to the thirty-eighth parallel. This they have not done, but on the contrary have pressed the attack. . . In these circumstances I have ordered United States air and sea forces to give the Korean Government troops cover and support.

The attack upon Korea makes it plain beyond all doubt that Communism has passed beyond the use of subversion to conquer independent nations and will now use armed invasion and war. It has defied the orders of the Security Council of the United Nations issued to preserve international peace and security. . .

Accordingly I have ordered the Seventh Fleet to prevent any attack on Formosa*. . . The Seventh Fleet will see that this is done. . .

I have similarly directed acceleration in the furnishing of military assistance to the forces of France and the associated states in Indochina and the dispatch of a military mission to provide close working relations with those forces.

Announcement by President Truman in Congress, 27 June 1950

* Formosa = Taiwan

F N.S. Khrushchev's Comments on the Korean War

The North Koreans wanted to give a helping hand to their brethren who were under the heel of Syngman Rhee. Stalin persuaded Kim Il-sung to think it over. . . Kim returned to Moscow when he had worked everything out. . . Stalin had his doubts. He was worried that the Americans would jump in, but we were inclined to think that if the war were fought swiftly – and Kim Il-sung was sure it could be won swiftly – then intervention by the USA could be avoided.

Nevertheless Stalin decided to ask Mao Zedong's opinion about Kim Il Sung's suggestion. I must stress it wasn't Stalin's idea, but Kim Il-sung's. Kim was the initiator. Stalin, of course, didn't try to dissuade him. . . Mao Zedong also answered him affirmatively. He approved Kim Il Sung's suggestion and put forward the opinion that the USA would not intervene since the war would be an internal matter which the Korean people would decide for themselves.

From N.S.Khrushchev, *Khrushchev Remembers*, ed. E. Crankshaw (1971)

Questions

1 What recent events on the mainland of China does Source A seek to explain? From your own knowledge, how accurately does the source infer the causes of these events? **(3 marks)**

2 Using Source B, and your own knowledge, show how closely the arguments of the Chinese Communists on the post-war activities of the United States corresponded to those of Soviet Communists.
(3 marks)

3 Use Sources A and C, and your own knowledge, to explain the increasing note of urgency that crept into US policy statements on the Far East in 1950. **(5 marks)**

4 Contrast the different accounts given in Sources D and E of the start of the Korean War. Which seems the more reliable, and why? **(7 marks)**

5 a) Use Sources D, E and F to explain whether, in your view, Source F is closer in agreement with Source D or Source E. **(6 marks)**
   b) Why might historians regard Source F as the least reliable of the five Sources A–F? **(6 marks)**

6 THE UNITED NATIONS AND THE KOREAN WAR

At the time it was widely believed that the Soviet Union was the main instigator of the North Korean invasion of South Korea, and the charge has been repeated many times since. Almost from the beginning, however, there have been those who have put forward reasons for doubting this interpretation. Their revelations, when published, have nearly always created the sort of sensation that suggests that previous *exposés* have never entirely registered.

There is a good deal of evidence to suggest that the war started because Syngman Rhee and Kim Il Sung were no longer willing to accept a divided nation; that both behaved provocatively towards the other until one of them launched a major attack; that the war, originally at least, was a civil war. But this was not the version that gained acceptance in the West. In Washington and London there was no doubt that it was Stalin who had hatched this plot to spread the Cold War to the Far East, and to extend the Soviet 'empire' there.

A few weeks before the war began, the Russians had walked out of the Security Council in protest against the refusal of the Western powers to admit representatives of Communist China to membership. The US view, strongly endorsed by those who denounced earlier US policies in the Far East as being too 'soft' on communism, was that the Nationalist regime, now exiled to Taiwan, was the legitimate government of China, and the group that had seized power in Beijing were no more than a temporary *de facto* leadership. Though there was no reason why the Soviet delegation should not return to the Security Council, it did not do so. The Soviet view was that the illegal exclusion of Mao's delegation rendered all other activities of the Security Council illegal, so that they need not veto them; whilst the US view, backed by the Western powers, was that the absence of the USSR from the Council did not constitute a veto and so did not invalidate UN proposals. There seems to have been some justification for both viewpoints.

Until the appropriate files are made public it will not be possible to be certain about who bore the main responsibility for the Korean War. From the aggressive tone of the diplomatic note which the Truman Administration fired off at Moscow on 27 July 1950, and from the public announcement that was made of the decision by the United States to intervene in the dispute on behalf of South Korea – some hours before the reference of the problem to the United Nations – it seems likely that the USA had already decided to enter the struggle and to 'go it alone' if necessary. On the other hand, the military evidence suggests that the initiative lay with the North Korean government, who had seven divisions ready for combat and masses of other troops which could be brought into play at short notice; and that their troops were massively supported by Soviet T-34 tanks, Yak fighters and Ilyushin ground-attack bombers liberally supplied by the USSR. The weakness of their South Korean opponents and their enormous losses in the first few days of the war hardly suggests that they were the main instigators of the struggle.

Whatever the final verdict, the episode certainly produced a new low in the temperature of the Cold War. The most lasting consequence of the Security Council stalemate was the decision of the General Assembly, taken in the Uniting for Peace resolution finally accepted on 3 November 1950, that, if the Security Council was deadlocked and so failed to maintain peace, the General Assembly could, by a two-thirds majority vote, take action in its stead. To the present, however, there remains doubt whether a two-thirds majority in the Assembly would be effective in overriding a veto in the Security Council.

A Stalin's Attitude to the Korean War

Stalin . . . was anxious to avoid armed conflict with the West; and his strategic interest in Korea was only slight. (Korea has a ten-mile frontier with the USSR, whereas her frontier with Manchuria stretches over 500 miles.) Yet Stalin acted with an eye to his latent rivalry with Mao. Having so recently and scandalously misjudged the chances of the revolution in China, he was anxious to dispel the impression of political timidity he had given, and wanted to prove himself as daring a strategist of revolution as Mao.

.The risks seemed negligible. It was about two years since the Soviet occupation armies had left Northern Korea; and by the end of 1948 the American troops had withdrawn from the South. Moreover the Americans had declared they had no vital interest to defend in Korea and hinted that they considered the country 'expendable.' Stalin had, therefore, some reason to assume that what Kim Il Sung was starting was a local war that would not turn into a major international conflict. He discovered his error when the United States decided to intervene in Korea and called upon the United Nations to do likewise. He committed another blunder when the Americans brought the issue before the Security Council. The Soviet member of the Council could easily have blocked the American action by making use of his right of veto, to which he had had frequent recourse even on trivial occasions. Instead, he demonstratively walked out during its critical session, as Moscow had instructed him to do; and so the United States and its allies, taking advantage of the absence of the Russian delegate, passed a vote obliging all members of the United Nations to send their troops to Korea to fight against the Communists.

From Isaac Deutscher, *Stalin* (1966)

B The USA Asks for the 'Good Offices' of the USSR

The text of the Note actually delivered in Moscow was not made available. Had this been done, it would have been seen that Truman's 'olive branch' had been made as thorny as possible by those who drafted the note. The tone was not a friendly request for mutual co-operation in ending the conflict, nor did it even use the phrase 'good offices'. It had a rasping and peremptory tone. . .

The announcement in Washington that the President had asked for Moscow's 'good offices' led us all to imagine a communication couched in friendly terms, not a hectoring and humiliating demand. Whether Truman was aware of how the American note was phrased is not known. The reply, under the circumstances, was astonishingly mild, though Moscow would have been wiser if it had by some concrete proposal opened the way for peace talks. The reply made three points. The first was that 'in accordance with facts verified by the Soviet Government' the events taking place in Korea 'were provoked by an attack by forces of the South Korean authorities on border regions of North Korea. Therefore the responsibility for these events rests upon the South Korean authorities and upon those who stand behind their back.' The second was that the Soviet government had withdrawn its troops from Korea earlier than the American government had, 'and thereby confirmed its traditional principle of non-interference in the affairs of other states. And now as well the Soviet Government adheres to the principle of the impermissibility of interference by foreign powers in the internal affairs of Korea.' The third point was that the Soviet Government had not 'refused' to take part in meetings of the Security Council but had 'not been able to take part . . . inasmuch as, because of the position of the United States, China, a permanent member of the Security Council, has not been admitted to the Council, which has made it impossible for the Security Council to take decisions having legal force'.

From I.F. Stone, *The Hidden History of the Korean War* (1952)

C Soviet 'Responsibility' for the Korean War

Kremlin strategy was known to be conservative at this time and to be highly sceptical of 'adventuristic' moves, a factor which would have been especially important considering the fluid situation in the South. . . Indeed, the thesis of Kremlin direction cannot be squared with the fact that the Soviet Union opted to boycott the UN at precisely that time in protest against Taiwan's presence on the Security Council. If the Kremlin had planned the invasion, it is difficult to understand why they did not postpone the attack for one month until the Russian delegate would have been Chairman of the Security Council and could have frustrated any proposed moves until the North Koreans had defeated the ill-equipped South Korean Army. . .

Even Soviet propaganda was caught napping by the attack. Communist papers were scooped on the outbreak and had no ready story of explanation, an unlikely pass had the invasion been carefully planned.

A former member of the United States Military Government in Korea, analyzing these and other facts inconsistent with the Western thesis, concludes that the attack on South Korea was ordered by Kim Il Sung of North Korea, not only without instructions from Moscow, but without its knowledge. The immediate event triggering Kim's decision may have been the fact that three envoys sent to Seoul on 11 June to discuss unification had been arrested and probably shot. A new Russian arms shipment had recently arrived, Rhee had been repudiated at the polls and a bumper rice crop was waiting in the South for the first time since World War II.

Whatever the war's origin, it is very clear there were elements of genuine civil conflict in the Korean situation which gave it a dynamic of its own. . .

When the fighting broke out, a cable was sent by the UN Temporary Commission on Korea to the UN's Secretary General declaring that what looked like a full-scale civil war was in progress, but assessing no blame for the origin of the fighting, and even quoting the North Korean radio claim that the South Koreans had invaded during the night and were being pursued south.

D. Horowitz, The Free World Colossus (1965)

D Soviet Actions Over the UN Security Council

On the afternoon of 25 June, the Council adopted the US resolution condemning the armed attack on the Republic of Korea, demanding an immediate withdrawal and calling on all members to render every assistance to the United Nations in the execution of this resolution.

This resolution was possible only because the Soviet Government had been boycotting the Security Council for two months, because of its refusal to seat the delegate of Communist China. The Russian delegate was in New York and might have returned to veto action against North Korea, but he didn't. Why then did the Kremlin permit the North Koreans to move during its absence from the Security Council? Was there just a possibility that the North Koreans had taken the bit in their own teeth and marched without orders from Moscow, or without its knowledge? This possibility was excluded by our faith in the power and deep strategy of the Kremlin.

From D.F. Fleming, *The Cold War and its Origins*, Vol. II (1961)

Questions

1 Using Source A, and your own knowledge, examine the opinion that Stalin's policies over the Korean crisis in 1950 were a 'blunder'.
(6 marks)

2 According to Sources B, C and D, what reasons were there for considering the Soviet leadership less culpable for the 'blunder' than they are often supposed to have been? **(9 marks)**

3 Use the sources to show:
   a) how the resolutions of the Security Council on the Korean crisis have been differently described (Sources A and D). **(2 marks)**
   b) how the withdrawal of the Soviet delegate from the Security Council has been differently related to the crisis (Sources A–D).
   (7 marks)

4 How do all these sources illustrate the problems of using secondary sources to write a historical account that is accurate and unbiased?
(6 marks)

7 THE CRISES OF 1956

1955 brought a lightening of Cold War tensions. The imminent
prospect of a Chinese Communist attack on Quemoy and Matsu in
March, which provoked Dulles's frightening threat of a full-blooded
nuclear response, in a paradoxical way helped towards the reduction
of tension by unveiling the grim vision of a nuclear holocaust, and
inclined world leaders towards negotiation instead of destruction. In
February 1955 the powers had already agreed to the future neutrality
of Austria, and shortly afterwards Khrushchev and Bulganin, the new
rulers of Soviet Russia, visited Belgrade, apologized to Marshal Tito
for the long years of enmity that Stalin had inflicted on Yugoslavia
and confessed rather sheepishly that 'there was more than one road to
Socialism.'

The first of a series of summit conferences took place at Geneva in
July 1955. In practical terms it achieved little: Germany remained
disunited, and both sides agreed that the continuation of the *status quo*
was the most practical strategy for the future. The real importance of
the conference was the fact that after nine years of confrontation the
two sides were able to meet together and discuss the world's problems
in a civilized way. President Eisenhower came out of the encounter
well, his bluff camaraderie as a former wartime ally laying to rest the
Russian idea that the Americans were inflexible and belligerent.

Détente was further advanced as the result of the meeting of the
Twentieth Party Congress of the Soviet Communist Party in February
1956 at which Khrushchev astounded the delegates by his sensational
denunciation of Stalin's regime. This produced not only renewed
hopes in the West for 'peaceful co-existence' between East and West
and for a settlement of outstanding problems, but a surge of
optimism in eastern European countries that the harsh Soviet yoke
might soon be lifted.

This new Soviet 'liberalism' soon made itself felt in Poland, where
riots in Poznan in June 1956 brought the return to power of their
popular leader Gomulka, imprisoned in 1951 for 'Titoism'. These
events encouraged dissent in Hungary, whose government had long
been unpopular for its Stalinist methods. Reforming Communists
looked to Imre Nagy, a former Hungarian Prime Minister who
returned to office in October 1956 on the invitation of the new First
Secretary, Ernö Gerö. There was an immediate outburst of national
enthusiasm, bringing sporadic street violence. Political prisoners were
amnestied; there was talk of holding genuinely free elections under a
multi-party system, and of adopting a policy of 'non-alignment' and

quitting the Warsaw Pact. This step, more than anything, struck a blow at the political cohesion of eastern Europe. Nagy admitted non-communists into his government and negotiated a cease-fire between the insurgents and Soviet troops stationed in the country. The Russians agreed to a withdrawal, but almost immediately, taking advantage of the pre-occupation of the Western powers with the Suez crisis, returned in force to crush the city. In three days the Hungarian Rising was put down and Nagy was whisked off to Russia, where he was secretly tried and executed. The Western powers hesitated to put Dulles's ideas on 'roll-back' into operation. Eisenhower hated communism, but he hated war more. The United Nations protested in vain, and generally the Hungarians were left to their fate.

In the meantime, nationalism was also growing in Egypt. After he came to power, Nasser negotiated the withdrawal of British troops from the Suez Canal Zone, and went on to nationalize the Canal Company with a view to using its profits for the building of the Aswan High Dam. The British Prime Minister Eden, convinced that Nasser was a second Hitler, and the French, the other former main proprietors of the Canal, called a conference in August to set up a Suez Canal Users' Association to safeguard their interests, and brought the issue before the United Nations in October, only to find that the Soviet Union vetoed the Anglo-French proposals.

Whilst the Security Council were discussing the problem, Nasser's enemies were planning military action. In late October the Israelis, having obtained western assurances of support, unleashed an attack across the Sinai Desert and within hours had reached the east bank of the Canal. The USA proposed a motion in the Security Council calling on Israel to withdraw and inviting other powers to dissociate themselves from their action. Britain and France vetoed this resolution, and issued ultimata to Cairo and Tel Aviv requiring the withdrawal of troops to areas more than ten miles from the Canal, ostensibly to prevent any damage to it. Israel complied but, when Egypt refused, an Anglo-French force, which had already set out from Cyprus, landed at Port Said and began an advance along the Canal towards the Red Sea. Nasser appealed for immediate UN intervention, meanwhile blocking the Canal by sinking ships in it. The invasion brought a swift denunciation from Eisenhower and Dulles, and a mischievous Soviet offer to assist the Americans in dealing with the aggression, but Britain did not feel strong enough to stand up to world disapproval and complied with UN instructions. Shortly afterwards Israeli forces left Sinai, and Anglo-French forces began their withdrawal from Egypt.

The British and French saw this episode as a great humiliation and were especially bitter about the failure of their American allies to stand by their side. The Soviet Union exploited the situation to the full, using it to divert world attention from the repression taking place in Hungary. The main gainer was Nasser, whose aspirations to strengthen Egypt and promote himself as leader of the Arab world were considerably advanced by the whole affair.

A Soviet Attitudes to the Hungarian Rising

The Soviet Government's decision to come to the aid of the 'revolutionary forces struggling against reaction in Hungary' was, according to the published views of Soviet leaders the only 'correct' one in the circumstances prevailing at that time.

The Soviet Declaration of 30 October concerning the principles of development and future strengthening of friendship and cooperation between the Soviet Union and other 'socialist' states included this comment on the Soviet intervention: 'The Soviet Government, in common with the entire Soviet people, profoundly deplore the fact that developments in Hungary have led to bloodshed. At the request of the Hungarian People's Government, the Soviet Government agreed to the entry into Budapest of Soviet Army units, in order to help the Hungarian People's Army to restore order in the city . . . The defence of the Socialist gains of People's Democratic Hungary is today the chief and sacred obligation of the workers, peasants and intelligentsia of the entire Hungarian working people'.

On 23 November 1956 *Pravda*, in an editorial, commented as follows on the Soviet intervention: 'A Socialist state could not remain an indifferent observer of the bloody reign of Fascist reaction in People's Democratic Hungary. When everything settles down in Hungary, and life becomes normal again, the Hungarian working class, peasantry and intelligentsia will undoubtedly understand our actions better and judge them aright. We regard our help to the Hungarian working class in its struggle against the intrigues of counter-revolution as our international duty.'

From the UN Report of the Special Committee on the Problem of Hungary, January 1957, paragraphs 103–105

B The US Attitude to the Hungarian Rising

I have noted with profound distress the reports which have reached me from Hungary. The declaration of the Soviet Government of 30 October 1956, which restates the policy of non-intervention in the internal affairs of other States, was generally understood as promising the early withdrawal of Soviet forces from Hungary. Indeed, in that statement the Soviet Union said that it considered the further presence of Soviet Army units in Hungary 'can serve as a cause for an even greater deterioration of the situation.' This pronouncement was regarded by the US

Government and myself as an act of high statesmanship. It was followed by the express request of the Hungarian Government for the withdrawal of Soviet forces.

Consequently, we have been inexpressibly shocked by the apparent reversal of this policy. It is especially shocking that this renewed application of force against the Hungarian Government and people took place while negotiations were going on between your representatives and those of the Hungarian Government for the withdrawal of Soviet forces.

As you know, the Security Council has been engaged in an emergency examination of this problem. As late as yesterday afternoon the Council was led to believe by your representative that the negotiations then in progress in Budapest were leading to agreement which would result in the withdrawal of Soviet forces from Hungary, as requested by the Government of that country. It was on that basis that the Security Council recessed* its consideration of this matter.

I urge in the name of humanity and in the cause of peace that the Soviet Union take action to withdraw Soviet forces from Hungary immediately, and to permit the Hungarian people to enjoy and exercise the human rights and fundamental freedoms affirmed for all peoples in the UN Charter.

Letter of President Eisenhower to Marshal Bulganin, 5 November 1956

* recessed = postponed

C The US Attitude to the Anglo-Franco-Israeli Action in the Suez Crisis
I doubt whether any delegate ever spoke from this forum with as heavy a heart as I have brought here tonight. We speak on a matter of vital importance, where the USA finds itself unable to agree with the three nations with whom it has ties, deep friendship, admiration and respect, and two of whom constitute our oldest, most trusted and reliable allies. . .

Surely we must feel that the peaceful processes which the Charter requests every member to follow had not been exhausted. . . I would be the last to say that there can never be circumstances where resort to force may not be employed, and certainly there can be resort to force for defensive purposes under Article 51. It seems to us that, under the circumstances which I have described, the resort to force, the violent armed attack by three of our members upon a fourth, cannot be treated other than as a grave error inconsistent with the principles and purposes of the Charter, and one which, if persisted in, would gravely undermine our Charter and this Organization. . .

If we do not act, and act promptly, and if we do not have sufficient unanimity of opinion so that our recommendations carry a real influence, there is a great danger that what is started, and what has been called a police action, may develop into something far more grave. Even if that does not happen, the apparent impotence of this Organization to deal with this situation may set a precedent which will lead other nations to attempt to take into their own hands the remedying of what they believe to be their own injustices. If that happens, the future is dark indeed.

Secretary of State J.F. Dulles, addressing the UN General Assembly,
1 November 1956

D Soviet Attitudes to the Anglo-French Invasion of Egypt

The Soviet Government considers it necessary to draw your attention to the aggressive war which is being waged by Britain and France against Egypt, which has the most dangerous consequences for the cause of general peace.

The special session of the General Assembly adopted a resolution for the immediate cessation of hostilities and the withdrawal of foreign troops from Egyptian territory. Ignoring this, Britain, France and Israel are intensifying their military actions, continuing their barbaric bombardment of Egyptian towns and villages, and landing troops on Egyptian territory. The British Government, together with France and Israel, have thus embarked on a path of unprovoked aggression against Egypt.

The reasons given by Britain to justify the aggression are completely unacceptable. The British Government declared that it had intervened in the Israeli-Egyptian conflict to prevent the Suez Canal Zone from becoming a theatre of hostilities. With the Anglo-French intervention, the Suez Canal Zone has become a theatre of war. . .

It cannot be concealed that an aggressive war is being waged against the Arab peoples, against the national independence of the states of the Near and Middle East, for the purpose of restoring the regime of colonial slavery rejected by those peoples. Nothing can justify the fact that the armed forces of France and Britain – two great powers, both permanent members of the Security Council – have attacked a country which only recently gained its independence and which does not have sufficient means for its defence.

In what position would Britain have found herself if she had been attacked by more powerful states possessing every kind of modern destructive weapon? There are countries which need not have sent a navy or air force to the shores of Britain but could have used other means, such as rocket techniques. If rocket weapons had been used against Britain and France, they would probably have called it a barbarous action. Yet in what ways does the inhuman attack made by the armed forces of Britain and France differ from this? . . .

The Soviet Government has approached the United States with a proposal to use naval and air forces, together with other UN members, to stop the war in Egypt and to restrain aggression. We are fully determined to crush the aggressors and restore peace in the East through the use of force. We hope at this critical moment you will display due prudence and draw the corresponding conclusions from this.

Letter of Marshal Bulganin to the British Prime Minister, Sir Anthony Eden, 5 November 1956

E British Response to Soviet Protests over Suez.
I have received with deep regret your message of yesterday. The language which you used in it made me think at first that I could only instruct Her Majesty's Ambassador to return it as entirely unaceptable. But the moment is so grave that I feel I must try to answer you with those counsels of reason with which you and I have in the past been able to discuss issues vital for the whole world. . .

If your Government will support proposals for an international force whose functions will be to prevent the resumption of hostilities between Israel and Egypt, to secure the withdrawal of the Israeli forces, to take the necessary measures to remove obstructions and restore traffic through the Suez Canal, and to promote a settlement of the problems of the area, you will be making a contribution which we would welcome.

Our aim is to find a peaceful solution, not to engage in argument with you. But I cannot leave unanswered the baseless accusations in your message. You accuse us of waging war against the national independence of the countries of the Near and Middle East. We have already proved the absurdity of this charge by declaring our willingness that the United Nations should take over the physical task of maintaining peace in the area.

You accuse us of barbaric bombardment of Egyptian towns and villages. Our attacks on airfields and other military targets have been conducted with the most scrupulous care in order to cause the least possible loss of life. Some casualties there must have been. We deeply regret them. When all fighting has ceased it will be possible to establish the true figure. We believe they will prove to be small. They will in any event be in no way comparable with the casualties which have been and still are being inflicted by the Soviet forces in Hungary.

The world knows that in the past three days Soviet forces in Hungary have been ruthlessly crushing the heroic resistance of a truly national movement for independence, a movement which by declaring its neutrality, proved that it offered no threat to the security of the Soviet Union.

At such a time it ill becomes the Soviet Government to speak of the actions of Her Majesty's Government as 'barbaric'. The United Nations have called on your Government to desist from all armed attack on the peoples of Hungary, to withdraw its forces from Hungarian territory, and to accept United Nations observers in Hungary. The world will judge from your reply the sincerity of the words which you have thought fit to use about Her Majesty's Government.

Letter of Sir Anthony Eden to Marshal Bulganin, 6 November 1956

Questions

1 a) How consistent are the two authorities quoted in Source A with what you know of Soviet communist pronouncements in the years after 1946? **(4 marks)**

b) Assess the reliability of Source A as historical evidence.

(3 marks)

2 What features of Sources B and C would lead you to the conclusion that the United States in 1956 was more understanding of British and French actions in Egypt than it was of Soviet actions in Hungary? **(3 marks)**

3 a) Why might the British Government have felt itself threatened by Marshal Bulganin's words in Source D? **(3 marks)**

b) Use Sources D and E to show how Soviet views on the Anglo-French invasion of Egypt in 1956 differed from the British view.

(4 marks)

c) How effectively, in your view, did Sir Anthony Eden make use of the Soviet suppression of the Hungarian Rising in his response (Source E) to Marshal Bulganin's letter? **(3 marks)**

4 Use the sentiments expressed in all the Sources A–E to illustrate the truth of N.S. Khrushchev's view that 'there are no neutral men'.

(10 marks)

8 THE BERLIN WALL

There was some improvement in the international situation at the end
of the 1950s. In particular, Khrushchev, plagued by the steadily-
increasing flow of emigrants from East Germany through Berlin,
began to ask for the conclusion of a peace treaty with Germany. The
death of J.F. Dulles in April 1959 increased the chances of negotiating
a settlement, and in September Khrushchev visited Eisenhower at the
President's rural retreat at Camp David in the Maryland hills where
the two men agreed that the matter 'should be settled not by the
application of force but by peaceful means through negotiation'. The
two agreed to another summit meeting in Paris in May 1960.

Unfortunately, shortly before the leaders met, it was announced
that an American U2 spy plane had been shot down over the Soviet
Union whilst on an espionage mission taking high-altitude
photographs, and that its pilot had been detained. Eisenhower
claimed (and in private Khrushchev believed him) that he had known
nothing of the affair, and later in Paris promised that such flights
should be cancelled. But in public Khrushchev would not be pacified,
and, according to the memoirs of the British Premier, Harold
Macmillan, 'to Western suggestions that this should satisfy Moscow,
he replied "That's a lackey's way. When a gentleman slaps a lackey's
face and then gives him as sixpence, the lackey at once says thank
you. . . But we know who we are and whom we represent."'

Nevertheless Khrushchev went to Paris for the summit only to find
it was now the turn of the Americans to be intransigent.

By the time J.F. Kennedy became US President at the beginning of
1961, Khrushchev was already beginning to threaten a unilateral
peace treaty with East Germany. The Russians also reverted to their
earlier intention of withdrawing their occupation forces from East
Berlin, claiming this as an act of military disengagement. More
important, it would force the Western powers to negotiate directly
with the East German government over the question of access to the
city. This was potentially embarrassing, since none of the Western
powers as yet recognized the DDR. Kennedy made it clear that he
would use force if necessary to preserve the *status quo* in Berlin. The
USA rushed through a number of defence measures. The USSR took
this as a counter-threat to themselves, and imposed restrictions in
Western air corridors to and from the city, and on canal traffic. Rail
traffic between the sectors of the city was also restricted, and the
Soviet authorities tightened their efforts to check migration of
refugees into West Berlin. This activity culminated in mid-August in

the final closure of the border and the building of the Berlin Wall between the eastern and western halves of the city.

The wall increased tension in the city, but at the same time provided the West with a cheap propaganda victory at the expense of a utopian socialist state that was forced to build a barrier to prevent its grateful citizens from running away. The DDR, still striving for Western recognition, continued into the autumn to create difficulties and delays at cross-points in the city, either to compel Khrushchev to come to their assistance, or else to test Western nerve. Tension was still running high two years later, when Kennedy visited the city and made his famous 'Ich bin ein Berliner' speech to the assembled crowds.

A A US View of the Berlin Enclave in 1960

The Berlin enclave was intolerable to the East [because of] the offence which West Berlin was to the communist East. It was a glittering outpost of capitalism, luxurious by comparison, prosperous, bustling. The United States had poured $600m into West Berlin. West Germany had also contributed heavily to make it a shining example of our way of life. . .

The economic comparison was damaging enough, but the comparison between the individual liberties in West Berlin and the regimented, tight police controls around it was still worse. The contrast led 300,000 East Germans each year to disappear into West Berlin and be flown out to West Germany. Mostly they were young, talented, educated and professional people – a drain which could not be endured indefinitely, unless East Germany was to be colonized by Russians and Poles. Since 1949 three million people had gone through the Berlin escape hatch and the population was declining. The magnet worked constantly.

West Berlin also contained the greatest combination of espionage agencies ever assembled in one place. It was an almost unbelievable windfall to be able to pursue all the missions of modern 'intelligence' agencies, including sabotage, 110 miles deep in 'the enemy's' territory. The same advantage accrued to Western radio stations and all other propaganda arms.

For all these reasons West Berlin was a deep running sore to the East, to be excised if at all possible. The only reason for surprise was that the second Berlin crisis had been postponed so long.

From D.F. Fleming, *The Cold War and Its Origins*, Vol. II, 1961

B Kennedy's Attitude towards the Berlin Situation

Our presence in West Berlin, and our access thereto, cannot be ended by any act of the Soviet Government. The NATO shield was long ago extended to cover West Berlin, and we have given our word that an attack upon that city will be regarded as an attack upon us all. For West Berlin, lying exposed 110 miles inside East Germany, surrounded by Soviet troops and close to the Soviet supply lines, has many roles. It is more than a showcase of liberty, a symbol, an island of freedom in a Communist sea; and more than a link with the free world, a beacon of hope behind the Iron Curtain, an escape hatch for refugees. West Berlin is all that. But above all it has become, as never before, the great testing place of Western courage and will; a focal point where our solemn commitments, stretching back over the years since 1945, and Soviet ambitions now meet in basic confrontation. . .

We cannot and will not permit the Communists to drive us out of Berlin, either gradually or by force. The fulfilment of our pledge to that city is essential to the morale and security of West Germany, to the unity of western Europe, to the faith of the entire free world. . .

The Atlantic Community . . . has been built in response to challenges: the challenge of European chaos in 1947; of the Berlin blockade in 1948; of Communist aggression in Korea in 1950. Now, standing strong and prosperous after an unprecedented decade of progress, the Atlantic Community will not forget either its history or the principles which gave it meaning. The solemn vow each of us gave to West Berlin in time of peace will not be broken in time of danger.

Broadcast by President Kennedy, 25 July 1961

C Soviet Response to Western Attitudes over the Berlin Question
For many years the United States has been evading a peaceful settlement with Germany, putting it off to the indefinite future. The American Note shows that the US Government prefers to continue adhering to this line.

Before everyone's eyes Western Germany is becoming a seat of war danger in Europe. A Regular Army headed by former Hitler generals and officers has sprung up there. Today, Western Germany has the largest army on the European continent among all the NATO member-countries. Representatives of the German Federal Republic hold key posts in NATO. . . The *Bundeswehr* is being formed and trained as an army designed to wage a rocket-nuclear war. . .

It is said that in Western Germany there is now no führer named Hitler. But do names determine the course of events? The course of events is influenced by people. And in Western Germany there are would-be führers galore. The population of Western Germany lives in an atmosphere of rampant revanchist* passions. The Government of the Federal Republic of Germany again and again advocates demands for the revision of the existing frontiers. . .

It is easy to imagine what language the West German militarists would be using were they to get nuclear weapons in their hands, which the Western powers seem to be willing to assist. How can the Soviet Government, remembering the devastating invasion of the Hitler hordes, ignore the fact that preparations are again being made in Western Germany? . . .

The Soviet Reply to Western Notes on Berlin, 3 August 1961

* revanchist = revengeful

D Khrushchev on the Berlin Question
In his recent speech [of 25 July] the President of the United States said that the USA faced a challenge of some kind from the Soviet Union, that there was a threat to the freedom of the people of West Berlin, that the Soviet Union was all but ready to use force. . .

What provisions of the Soviet draft of a peace treaty with Germany could give the American President a pretext to contend that the Soviet Union 'threatens' to violate peace? Could it be those which envisage the renunciation of nuclear weapons by Germany, the legalising of the existing German frontiers, the granting of full sovereignty to both German states, and by their admission to the United Nations?

If anyone allowed himself to resort to threats it was the US President. He did not stop at presenting us with an ultimatum in reply to the proposal to conclude a peace treaty with Germany. As if to reinforce his threats, the President announced an increase in the strength of the US armed forces by 217,000 men.

N.S. Khrushchev, in a television broadcast, 7 August 1961

E Contemporary Report on the Building of the Wall
During the night of 17–18 August a concrete barrier up to 6ft high and topped with barbed wire . . . was erected in the Potsdamerplatz by Communist 'shock workers'; similar concrete barriers were raised at other points along the sector boundaries, apparently designed to fill in existing gaps between crossing points.

In a broadcast on 18 August, Herr Ulbricht said that the sealing-off of East Berlin would 'facilitate the conclusion of a peace treaty and the solution of the West German problem', rejected Western charges that the measures constituted a breach of existing treaties, and counter-charged that the Western powers had themselves broken those treaties by setting up the 'militaristic clique' in Bonn in 1949. Speaking of 'our dear brothers and sisters, the West German people', Herr Ulbricht expressed 'regret' that they had allowed their government to 'fall into the hands of Fascists, Nazis, militarists, warmongers, slave traders and head hunters'.

From *Keesings Contemporary Archives*, report of 23 August 1961

F Khrushchev's Recollections of Confrontations at the Berlin Wall
Marshal Konev [Soviet Commander in East Berlin] reported that he had
learned through intelligence channels on what day and at what hour the
Western powers were going to begin their actions against us. They
were preparing bulldozers to break down our border installations. The
bulldozers would be followed by tanks and wave after wave of jeeps
with infantrymen. . .

We went into consultation and worked out in advance what our
response would be. We concentrated our own infantry units in the side
streets near the checkpoints along the border. We also brought in our
tanks at night and stationed them nearby. Then there was nothing for us
to do but wait and see what the West would do next.

Then Konev reported that the American bulldozers, tanks and jeeps
had moved out and were heading in the direction of our checkpoints.
Our men did not move, even when the bulldozers moved right up to the
border. Then all at once our tanks rolled out of the side streets and
moved forward to meet the American tanks. . .

The tanks and troops of both sides spent the night lined up facing
each other across the border. It was late October and chilly. . .

I proposed that we turn our tanks around, pull them back from the
border and have them take their places in the side streets. Then we
would wait and see what happened next. . . I said that I thought the
Americans would pull back their tanks within twenty minutes after we
had removed ours. This was how long it would take their tank
commander to report our move and get orders from higher up of what
to do.

Konev ordered our tanks to pull back from the border. He reported
that just as I expected, it did take only twenty minutes for the Americans
to respond.

Thus the West tested our nerve by prodding us with the barrels of
their cannons and found us ready to accept their challenge. They
learned they couldn't frighten us. I think it was a great victory for us, and
it was won without firing a single shot.

N.S. Khrushchev, in *Khrushchev Remembers*, ed. E. Crankshaw, 1971

G President Kennedy and the West Berlin People
Two thousand years ago the proudest boast in the world was *Civis
Romanus Sum*. Today, in the world of freedom, the proudest boast is
Ich bin ein Berliner.

There are many people in the world who do not understand what is
the great issue between the free world and Communism. Let them
come to Berlin. And there are some who say in Europe and elsewhere
that we can work with the Communists. Let them come to Berlin.

Freedom has many difficulties and democracy is not perfect; but we never had to put up a wall to keep our people in. I know of no city which has been besieged for 18 years and still lives with the vitality, force, hope and determination of this city of West Berlin. While the wall is the most obvious and vivid demonstration of the failures of the Communist system, we take no satisfaction in it, for it is an offence not only against history but against humanity. . .

In 18 years of peace and good faith this generation of Germans has earned the right to be free, including the right to unite their family and nation in lasting peace with the goodwill of all people. When the day finally comes when this city will be joined as one in this great continent of Europe, the people of West Berlin can take great satisfaction in the fact that they were in the front line for almost two decades.

President J.F. Kennedy, in a speech in West Berlin, 26 June 1963

Questions

1 Why, according to Source A, did Western commentators consider that West Berlin was an 'almost intolerable offence' to the Communist East? **(4 marks)**

2 Use Sources B and C to illustrate the different views taken by the USA and the USSR of the causes of the Berlin crisis in 1961. **(5 marks)**

3 Use Sources B, C and D, and your own judgment, to assess which of the two sides, East and West, behaved in a more threatening way to its opponent in 1961. **(5 marks)**

4 In what way do Sources E and F differ from Source G in their feelings on the subject of the Berlin Wall? **(4 marks)**

5 a) How consistent are the opinions expressed in Source D with those expressed by the same author in Source F? **(4 marks)**
   b) Which of the two in your estimation provides the most reliable measure of Khrushchev's opinion on the subject, and why? **(8 marks)**

9 THE CUBAN MISSILES CRISIS, 1962

No sooner had the crisis over the Berlin Wall and the whole future of Germany begun to simmer down than tension boiled up again. The new crisis was in the Caribbean – much nearer to home for the United States.

The long-running guerrilla war taking place in the mountains of eastern Cuba culminated at the end of 1958 in the flight of the former Cuban dictator Fulgencio Batista to Dominica, and as a result the radical law-student Fidel Castro, who had led the campaign to free his country from tyranny, found himself at the age of 32 the new ruler of the island. The radical tendencies of his new government were soon evident. Land was seized and distributed to the peasants, large measures of state control were enacted and strenuous efforts were made to clear up the vice and corruption for which Cuba was notorious. Castro embarked on a policy of nationalizing US-owned enterprises, confiscating over $1 billion of US investments in the island. His egalitarian policies and their vocabulary of Marxist jargon soon seemed to threaten the creation of a Communist dictatorship on the Caribbean doorstep of the USA, and though Khrushchev regarded him as more of a nationalist than a fully-fledged communist, the US Administration quickly made up its mind to be rid of him.

When J.F. Kennedy became President of the USA in 1961 he inherited a CIA plot to send in a small army of anti-Castro volunteers to overthrow the new regime. Unfortunately for the new president's reputation, Castro's jets shot down the air cover of the 1500-strong force within hours and then mopped up the insurgent army. The whole 'Bay of Pigs' episode was intensely embarrassing for the United States.

Worse was to follow. In October 1962 an American U2 spy-plane brought back aerial photographs showing that Castro was constructing sites for intermediate range ballistic missiles (IRBMs). If these were equipped with nuclear warheads every US city within 4000km (nearly all of them) and many cities in Latin and South America would be in danger of nuclear attack. It did not take US Intelligence long to discover that Soviet advisers were directing the whole operation and Soviet suppliers providing the hardware. On 23 October Kennedy proclaimed an immediate blockade of Cuba and the imposition of what he called a 'strict quarantine' on all offensive equipment under shipment. For several anxious days Washington and the rest of the world were on red alert. Khrushchev reacted angrily, but was not prepared to risk all-out nuclear war, and ordered

Russian ships to turn for home. Both sides represented the outcome as a victory, but world opinion generally agreed with the US official who said 'We were eyeball to eyeball, but I think the other fellow just blinked.'

The crisis had important results. In its wake a 'hot line' telephone and telex link was set up between the White House and the Kremlin to help avert similar crises in future – and to avert an accidental nuclear outbreak caused by faulty intelligence or malfunctioning electronic equipment. On the Russian side came the dismissal of Khrushchev in October 1964 by a hawkish group in the Politburo who regarded his sensible caution as weakness. The Americans, for their part, realized that something positive had to be done to check the spread of Castroism; here the role of the Alliance for Progress between the United States and the developing economies of Latin America was of great importance.

A Proclamation of the Cuban Blockade, October 1962

Whereas the peace of the world and the security of the United States and of all American states are endangered by reason of the establishment by the Sino-Soviet powers of an offensive military capability in Cuba, including bases for ballistic missiles with a potential range covering most of North and South America;

And whereas the Organ of Consultation of the American Republics meeting in Washington on October 23rd 1962, recommended that the member states, in accordance with Articles 6 and 8 of the Inter-American Treaty of Reciprocal Assistance, take all measures, individually and collectively, including the use of armed force, which they may deem necessary to insure that the Government of Cuba cannot continue to receive from the Sino-Soviet powers military material and related supplies. . .

I, John F. Kennedy, President of the United States of America . . . do hereby proclaim that the forces under my command are ordered beginning at 2pm Greenwich time October 24th 1962, to interdict . . . the delivery of offensive weapons and associated material to Cuba. . .

To enforce this order, the Secretary of Defense shall take appropriate measures to prevent the delivery of prohibited material to Cuba, employing the land, sea and air forces of the United States. . .

The Secretary of Defense may make such regulations and issue such directives as he deems necessary to ensure the effectiveness of this order, including the designation, within a reasonable distance of Cuba, of prohibited or restricted zones and of prescribed routes.

Any vessel or craft which may be proceeding toward Cuba may be intercepted and may be directed to identify itself, its cargo, equipment and stores and its ports of call, to stop, lie to, or submit to visit and search, or to proceed as directed. Any vessel or craft which fails or refuses to respond or to comply with directions shall be subjected to being taken into custody.

Proclamation by President Kennedy of a Blockade of Cuba, 23 October 1962

B   US Intelligence Photograph of Soviet Missile Sites in Cuba, 1962

C Soviet Vessel *Asonov* returning to Russia carrying missiles, November 1962

D President Kennedy's Attitude towards the Cuban Crisis

President Kennedy dedicated himself to making it clear to Khrushchev by word and deed . . . that the United States had limited objectives and that we had no intention of accomplishing those objectives by adversely affecting the national security of the Soviet Union or by humiliating her. . .

During our crisis talks he kept stressing the fact that we would indeed have war if we placed the Soviet Union in a position she believed would adversely affect her national security or such public humiliation that she lost the respect of her own people and countries round the globe. The missiles in Cuba, we felt, vitally concerned our national security, but not that of the Soviet Union.

This fact was ultimately recognized by Khrushchev, and this recognition, I believe, brought about this change in what, up to that time, had been a very adamant position. The President believed from the start that the Soviet Chairman was a rational, intelligent man, who if given sufficient time and shown our determination, would alter his position. But there was always the chance of error, of mistake, miscalculation, or misunderstanding, and President Kennedy was committed to do everything possible to lessen that chance on our side.

From Senator Robert Kennedy, *Thirteen Days*, (1969)

E Khrushchev's Recollection of the Cuba Crisis

After Castro's crushing victory over the counter-revolutionaries we intensified our military aid to Cuba. . . We were quite sure that the Americans would never reconcile themselves to the existence of Castro's Cuba. They feared, as much as we hoped, that a socialist Cuba might become a magnet that would attract other Latin American countries to socialism. Given the continual threat of American interference in the Caribbean, what should our own policy be? . . .

The fate of Cuba and the maintenance of Soviet prestige in that part of the world preoccupied me. . . We had to establish a tangible and effective deterrent to American interference in the Caribbean. But what exactly? The logical answer was missiles. We knew that American missiles were aimed against us in Turkey and Italy, to say nothing of West Germany. . .

I had the idea of installing missiles with nuclear warheads in Cuba without letting the United States find out they were there until it was too late to do anything about them. . .

I want to make one thing absolutely clear: when we put our ballistic missiles in Cuba, we had no desire to start a war. On the contrary, our principal aim was to deter America from starting a war. . .

The climax came after five or six days when our Ambassador to Washington, Anatoly Dobrynin, reported that the President's brother, Robert Kennedy, had come to see him on an unofficial visit. Dobrynin's report went something like this:

'Robert Kennedy looked exhausted. . . He said that he had not been home for six days and nights. "The President is in a grave situation", Robert Kennedy said, "and he does not know how to get out of it. We are under very severe stress . . . from our military to use force against Cuba. . . We want to ask you, Mr Dobrynin, to pass President Kennedy's message to Chairman Khrushchev through unofficial channels. President Kennedy implores Chairman Khrushchev to accept his offer and to take into consideration the peculiarities of the American system. . . If the situation continues much longer, the President is not sure that the military will not overthrow him and seize power. The American army could get out of control."'

I hadn't overlooked this possibility. We knew that Kennedy was a young President and that the security of the United States was indeed threatened. . .

We sent the Americans a note saying that we agreed to remove our missiles and bombers on the condition that the President give us his assurance that there would be no invasion of Cuba by the forces of the United States or anybody else. Finally Kennedy gave in and agreed to make a statement giving us such an assurance. . .

It had been, to say the least, an interesting and challenging situation. The two most powerful nations in the world had been squared off against each other, each with its finger on the button. . . It was a great victory for us, though. . .

The Caribbean crisis was a triumph of Soviet foreign policy and a personal triumph in my own career. . . We achieved, I would say, a spectacular success without having to fire a single shot!

From N.S. Khrushchev, *Khrushchev Remembers*, ed. E Crankshaw, 1971

Questions

1 a) What US responses were suggested by President Kennedy in Source A to deal with the Cuban Missiles crisis in 1962?

(4 marks)

   b) What features of Source A show that Kennedy was determined not to be seen acting unilaterally in the crisis? **(4 marks)**

2 What evidence is there in Source D of a US willingness to act moderately over the Cuban crisis? **(4 marks)**

3 What evidence is there in Source E of a comparable moderation on the part of the Soviet leader? **(5 marks)**

4 In what ways do the explanations of developments during the Cuban Missiles crisis given in Sources D and E differ from one another? **(8 marks)**

5 What light is cast by Sources D and E on the reliability of the memoirs of statesmen as historical evidence? Refer in your answer both to Source D and to Source E. **(6 marks)**

6 For what purposes were the photographs in Sources B and C originally taken? **(3 marks)**

7 Referring to Sources B and C, and to other photographs with which you may be familiar, comment on the value of photographs as historical evidence. **(6 marks)**

10 THE WAR IN VIETNAM

When the French returned to their former colony of Indochina in 1946, they faced a war in North Vietnam against the nationalist Vietminh, led by Ho Chi Minh, a resistance leader who had built up socialist cells and survived in turn the attentions of the Japanese and the Chinese Nationalists. After eight years of fighting, Ho succeeded in defeating the French at Dien Bien Phu. A conference at Geneva followed in the summer of 1954, dividing the whole country into four new states: Laos and Cambodia were to be neutralized, and Vietnam was to be sub-divided into North and South, their boundary a demilitarized zone along the 17th Parallel. Elections were to be held there after two years to reunite the country, which in the meanwhile remained under Ho and his communist followers in the North and under former Emperor Bao Dai in the South.

Thereafter, the Americans came to play an increasingly important part in Vietnam. To Eisenhower, and later to Kennedy, Vietnam, a border state between the communist and the non-communist spheres of influence, was a bastion of the 'free world'. Both Presidents saw the relevance of the 'domino principle' to the situation there. The newly-established Republic of Vietnam, set up in the South under the Catholic aristocrat Ngo Dinh Diem, was increasingly supported by United States money and expertise. His policies became repressive, particularly of local Buddhist opinion, and on his assassination in November 1963 the country passed under military government. At the outset of Kennedy's presidency there had been fewer than 700 US servicemen in Vietnam, but by 1965 this number had swelled to about half a million, and the USA found itself committed to propping up a country rapidly crumbling under nationalist and communist pressures.

President Johnson found himself in a bitter struggle which he could not end either by victory or by negotiation; the harder he struggled, the more deeply he became involved. It distracted him from an ambitious programme of domestic reforms, and ultimately it led to his decision to stand down from the Presidency in 1968. As one of the last acts of his Presidency he halted the bombing of North Vietnam; his successor, Richard Nixon, opened peace talks in Paris, and sought to reduce US commitments in the country by a process of *Vietnamization*, whereby he handed over responsibility for the war to the South Vietnamese themselves. Predictably, this policy failed, and unwittingly Nixon found himself sinking steadily into the same quagmire as Johnson. He launched massive air-strikes against the

North; only when this policy of 'bombing the enemy to the conference table' had been abandoned were the Paris negotiations renewed.

Eventually a cease-fire and a peace treaty were agreed in 1973 and rather unconvincingly presented to the US people as a victory. As a result, US troops were to leave Vietnam in two months, prisoners were to be exchanged and a UN truce-supervision force was to monitor the new arrangements. It was only a short time before North Vietnam completely overran the South and the country was reunited under communist leadership.

As an exercise in bolstering the South Vietnamese 'domino', the war had been a disastrous failure. Laos and Cambodia succumbed to the advancing tide, but generally the anticipated results did not follow. For one thing, the communist east was much less monolithic than it appeared: serious differences emerged between the Soviet Union and Communist China, and it was not long before China and Vietnam were actually at war over their disputed frontier. Brezhnev deeply disapproved of Deng Xiaoping's policies in South-east Asia and even tried to blame him for the hideous excesses of the Khmer Rouge in Kampuchea (Cambodia), though in fact Vietnamese intervention in that country came almost as a merciful deliverance from the barbarism of Pol Pot's regime. The success of communist insurgency, furthermore, was generally limited: it fared quite well when it fought with popular support against decadent post-colonialist regimes, but when it came up against stronger governments, or those commanding nationalist loyalties of their own, it achieved fewer successes.

A Principles of US Policy in the Far East
(i) The Origin of Eisenhower's 'Domino Principle'
2 Communist domination, by whatever means, of all South-east Asia would seriously endanger in the short term, and critically endanger in the longer term, United States security interests.

a The loss of any of the countries of South-east Asia to communist aggression would have critical psychological, political and economic consequences. In the absence of effective and timely counteraction, the loss of any single country would probably lead to relatively swift submission to or an alignment with communism by the remaining countries of this group. Furthermore, an alignment with communism of the rest of South-east Asia and India, and in the longer term, of the Middle East (with the probable exceptions of at least Pakistan and Turkey) would in all probability progressively follow. Such widespread alignment would endanger the stability and security of Europe.

b Communist control of all of South-east Asia would render the US position in the Pacific offshore islands precarious and would seriously jeopardize fundamental US security interests in the Far East.

  c South-east Asia, especially Malaya and Indonesia, is the principal world source of natural rubber and tin, and a producer of petroleum and other strategically important commodities. The rice exports of Burma and Thailand are critically important to Malaya, Ceylon and Hong Kong and are of considerable significance to Japan and India, all important areas of free Asia.

  d The loss of South-east Asia, especially of Malaya and Indonesia, could result in such economic and political pressures as to make it extremely difficult to prevent Japan's eventual accommodation to communism.

From NSC 124/2, June 1952, as quoted in the *Pentagon Papers* (pub. 1971)

(ii) President Kennedy on US Support for South Vietnam
Vietnam represents the cornerstone of the Free World in South-east Asia, the keystone to the arch, the finger in the dike. Burma, Thailand, India, Japan, the Philippines, and, obviously, Laos and Cambodia are among those whose security would be threatened if the red tide of communism overflowed into Vietnam. . . Moreover the independence of Free Vietnam is crucial to the free world in fields other than the military. Her economy is essential to the economy of all South-east Asia; and her political liberty is an inspiration to those seeking to obtain or maintain their liberty in all parts of Asia – and indeed the world. The fundamental tenets of this nation's foreign policy, in short, depend in considerable measure upon a strong and free Vietnamese nation.

President J.F. Kennedy, in a speech to the American Friends of Vietnam,
June 1956

B Ho Chi Minh on US Support for South Vietnam
So long as the US army of aggression still remains on our soil, our people will resolutely fight against it. If the US Government really wants a peaceful settlement, it must accept the four-point stand of the Democratic Republic of Vietnam Government and prove this by actual deeds; it must end unconditionally and for good all bombing raids and all other war acts against the DRV. Only in this way can a political solution to the Vietnam problem be envisaged. . .

  In the face of the extremely serious situation brought about by the United States in Vietnam, I firmly believe that the people and government of the fraternal [recipient country*] will extend increased support and assistance to our people's just struggle, resolutely condemn the US Government's sham peace tricks, and check in time all

new perfidious manoeuvres of the United States in Vietnam and
Indochina.

From a letter of Ho Chi Minh to the Heads of several other Governments,
24 January 1966

* i.e. South Vietnam

C President Johnson's Reflections on the Vietnam War

I think we have made two mistakes in Vietnam. . . First, our posture at
home and abroad may have been too moderate, too balanced, not
strong or assertive enough from the first. It is possible that we may have
moved into Vietnam too slowly; that we have been too restrained in our
bombing policy; too gradual across the board. In retrospect, we may
have been too cautious for too long. Second, we may have helped to
create mistrust or misinterpretation of our peace proposals. If the
sincerity of our peace overtures is questioned, it could be that we have
crawled* too often. History will record the lengthy and imaginative list
of US peace initiatives. It will record how they met nothing but arrogant
rebukes by North Vietnam. . . If gradualism does not pay off early, then
the enemy must be regarded as the enemy and fought with all
resources, with no sanctuary or quarter given.

L.B. Johnson's remarks in the White House to a visiting Australian group,
September 1967

* crawled = grovelled

D President Johnson's Decision of 1968

I would ask all Americans, whatever their personal interests or concern,
to guard against divisiveness and all its ugly consequences. . .

Our reward will come in the life of freedom, peace and hope that our
children will enjoy through ages ahead. . .

Believing this as I do, I have concluded that I should not permit the
Presidency to become involved in the partisan divisions that are
developing in this political year. . .

Accordingly, I shall not seek, and will not accept, the nomination of
my Party for another term as your President. And let men everywhere
know that a strong, a confident and a vigilant America stands ready
tonight to defend an honored cause – whatever the price, whatever the
burden, whatever the sacrifices that duty may require.

President Johnson's Broadcast to the Nation, 31 March 1968

The Train Robbery

E A British View of President Johnson's Vietnam Policies

F President Nixon Announces the End of the Vietnam War
At 12.30pm Paris time today, 23 January 1973, the agreement on ending the war and restoring the peace was initialled by Dr Henry Kissinger on behalf of the United States and by Le Duc Tho on behalf of the Democratic Republic of Vietnam. . .

The cease-fire will take effect at 24.00 GMT, 27 January 1973. . . The United States and the Democratic Republic of Vietnam express the hope that this agreement will secure stable peace in Vietnam and contribute to the preservation of lasting peace in Indochina and South-east Asia. . .

Throughout the years of negotiations we have insisted on peace with honour. . . In the settlement that has now been agreed to, all the conditions that I laid down then have been met. . .

Throughout these negotiations we have been in the closest consultation with President Thieu and other representatives of the Republic of Vietnam. This settlement meets the goals and has the full support of President Thieu. . .

The United States will continue to recognize the Government of the Republic of Vietnam as the sole legitimate government of South Vietnam. We shall continue to aid South Vietnam within the terms of the agreement, and we shall support efforts by the people of South Vietnam to settle their problems peacefully amongst themselves.

President Nixon's Broadcast to the Nation, 23 January 1973

G The Soviet View of China's Role in Vietnam After the War
An article published in *Pravda* on 28 February 1979, signed 'Igor Alexandrov' (a pseudonym used for semi-official statements) accused China of regarding the whole of South-east Asia as its sphere of influence. China, it alleged, had offered to send troops to North Vietnam during the war with the United States, while obstructing the delivery of Soviet military aid; it brought the Pol Pot regime to power in Cambodia; 'planned in detail the wholesale annihilation of the Cambodian people' as a step to 'Chinese assimilation of the temporarily devastated and enslaved Cambodia and its transformation into an important Chinese bridgehead for the encirclement of "disobedient" Vietnam, offering also direct access to Malaysia, Thailand and Indonesia'; and ordered the Pol Pot regime to attack Vietnam, in order 'to make Vietnam fight on two fronts at once'. 'The reaction of the US Administration to the Chinese aggression', the article continued, 'appears, if not as approval, then at least most definitely as indirect encouragement. . . The decision to start the invasion was taken by the Chinese leaders right after Deng Xiaoping's return from the USA. . . Beijing does not deny the connection between the timing of the aggression, the conclusion of the Sino-Japanese treaty and the "normalization" of Sino-American relations.'

In a speech on 2 March, President Brezhnev condemned China's policy as 'the most serious threat to peace in the whole world' and referred to 'the danger of any forms of connivance with that policy', but did not directly mention the United States in this connection.

Soviet Reactions to the Chinese Invasion of North Vietnam 1979, as reported in *Keesings Contemporary Archives*, October 1979

Questions

1 a) Explain why President Eisenhower later came to refer to the ideas set out in Source A(i) as the *Domino Principle*.   **(2 marks)**
   b) Show how, in Source A, President Kennedy was influenced by this principle.   **(3 marks)**

2 Referring to Sources B and C, show how the views of the Vietnam War held by North Vietnamese and US leaders differed from each other.   **(4 marks)**

3 a) Use Sources D and E, and your own knowledge, to trace the impact of the Vietnamese War on President Johnson's domestic problems.   **(4 marks)**
   b) Referring to Source E, and to any other examples with which you are familiar, explain the value of political cartoons as historical evidence.   **(6 marks)**

4 How do the tone and content of Sources C and F help to reveal the changed circumstances in the Vietnamese War in which the sources were produced?   **(5 marks)**

5 In what ways might Source G be used to show that the Communist East was 'less monolithic than it appeared'? How reliable is this Source as historical evidence?   **(6 marks)**

11 THE SINO-SOVIET DISPUTE

In 1950, Mao and Stalin signed a 30-year Treaty of Friendship and Alliance, under which the Russians provided much technical and financial assistance and a good deal of industrial expertise for the process of modernization. However, the Chinese communists were much less docile than the Soviet satellites in Europe: they expected a dominant role in Asia, frequently adopted a very independent line in their dealings with the Third World, felt themselves entitled to share in the USSR's nuclear secrets, and demanded more vigorous Soviet help in the conflict with Jiang Jieshi over the future of Taiwan.

The immediate cause of the breach between the two countries was the 20th Party Conference in 1956, at which Khrushchev made his first public criticism of Stalin. The honesty of his criticism struck a responsive chord in many Russian hearts, but it generated great resentment in China, where Mao saw himself in a Stalinist role. He accused Khrushchev of the same kind of 'deviationism' from true communist teaching as that for which Stalin had condemned many of his own opponents. Mao also resented Khrushchev's scepticism about the Great Leap Forward, and believed his decision to withdraw Soviet advisers from China in August 1960 was pettily vindictive. Further, in foreign affairs, Khrushchev's visits to the West, his discussions with Western leaders and his general tolerance of the West's styles of thinking – in particular his advocacy of 'live-and-let-live' as the basis of his new policy of *co-existence* – all seemed to Mao to be signs of the steady corruption of his ideals; he had lost his sense of direction, and was halfway to joining the ranks of the enemy.

The Sino-Soviet split came into the open at the Bucharest Conference in 1960 and was one of the factors leading directly to the fall of Khrushchev – indeed it was one of the main reasons why the hard-liners in the Soviet Politburo attacked him. The accession to power of Brezhnev and Kosygin in October 1964 made Sino-Soviet relations easier, but the renewal of negotiations between Moscow and Washington upset the Chinese once more and the quarrels broke out afresh. The Russian press denounced the Chinese, and they for their part bitterly complained of 'the anti-China atrocities of the new Tsars . . . their Fascist heel tramples the motherland.' In particular there were skirmishes on the Sino-Soviet border in Manchuria and elsewhere, the most serious confrontations being at several points along the Ussuri River, whose meandering course marked the ill-defined frontier. The Chinese strongly objected to the terms of the 'unequal treaties' inherited from the decadent Manchu, which deprived China of rights which they had enjoyed from time immemorial in neighbouring provinces. In the later 1960s the conflict along the frontier escalated almost into full-scale war.

Sino-Soviet ill-will could also be seen at the time of the Czechoslovak crisis in 1968, when the Soviet leader produced his *Brezhnev Doctrine* in which he set out a justification for direct action on the part of the Warsaw Pact in defence of communism similar to the doctrine which President Truman had set out earlier to justify US intervention against it. The Chinese leadership took this as unwarrantable interference with the rights of supposedly sovereign states to decide on their own policies, and drew a lurid picture of the men of the Kremlin as morally and ideologically indistinguishable from most of the imperialist West.

A The 20th Party Congress and the Cult of the Personality

(i) The 20th Congress of the CPSU is the origin of the split in the international communist movement. From the moment it took place, confusion arose within the movement and within the ranks of many Communist Parties. . . They are becoming deeper with each passing day because the CPSU leadership persists in pursuing the revisionist line of that Congress and insistently seeks to impose it on the fraternal parties of other countries.

The 20th Congress of the CPSU has greatly helped imperialism and the reactionaries of all countries by providing them with weapons against revolution, against communism and against the communist camp. . . In the past nine years, imperialism and its stooges have consistently made use of the revisionist line, formulated at this Congress and later developed and systematized, in order to undermine the international communist movement and the revolutionary cause of the peoples of all countries.

What Khrushchev and company did during and after the 20th Congress has shown that they have thoroughly betrayed the international proletariat and the revolutionary peoples of the world.

From publisher's preface to *Statements by Khrushchev*, Vol. V, World Culture Press, Beijing, 1965

(ii) The CPC leaders have taken on themselves the role of the defenders of the cult of the individual and disseminators of Stalin's erroneous ideas. They are trying to impose upon other parties the practice, the ideology and ethics, and the forms and methods of leadership which flourished in the period of the cult of individualism. We must say outright that this is an unenviable role which will bring them neither honour nor glory. No one will succeed in persuading the Marxist-Leninists and the progressive people to take the road of defending the cult of the individual!

The Soviet people and the world communist movement duly appreciated the courage, boldness and the truly Leninist firmness of principle demonstrated by our party and by its central committee headed by Nikita Khrushchev, in the struggle against the consequences of the cult of the individual.

From an Open Letter from the Central Committee of the CPSU, printed in *Pravda*, 14 July 1963

B Differences between the CPSU and the CPC at the Bucharest Conference, 1960

(i) At Bucharest, to our amazement, the leaders of the CPSU . . . unleashed a surprise assault on the Chinese Communist Party, turning the spearhead of the struggle against us and not against US imperialism.

The Bucharest meeting of representatives of fraternal parties took place 24–26 June 1960. It is a plain lie for the Open Letter of the CPSU to describe that meeting as 'comradely assistance' to the Chinese Communist Party. . .

In the meeting, Khrushchev took the lead in organizing a great converging onslaught on the Chinese Communist Party. In his speech he wantonly vilified the CCP as 'madmen', 'wanting to unleash war', 'picking up the banner of the imperialist monopoly capitalists'. . . Some of the fraternal Party representatives who obeyed Khrushchev and followed his lead also wantonly charged the CCP with being 'dogmatic', 'Left adventurist', 'pseudo-revolutionary', 'sectarian' and so on and so forth.

Editorial Departments of *People's Daily* and *Red Flag*, Beijing, 6 September 1963

(ii) If one is to look for real double-dealers and schismatics acting 'behind the backs of the fraternal parties', one must speak of those who have carried on factional activity for many years, and must go to those who openly argue for a split in the communist movement and declare it to be 'an inexorable law'. . .

This is nothing but the most real behind-the-scenes factional activity against a fraternal party. One could cite innumerable facts, and if necessary publish documents, that expose the behind-the-scenes activity of the CCP leadership against the CPSU and other fraternal parties.

From a letter to the Chinese Central Committee from the Soviet Central Committee, 22 February 1964, quoted in the *People's Daily*, 9 May 1964

C Conflict on the Sino-Soviet Border, 1962–64

(i) The Government of the People's Republic of China has consistently held that the question of the boundary between China and the Soviet Union, which is a legacy from the past, can be settled through negotiation between the two governments. . .

With the stepping up of anti-Chinese activities by the leaders of the CPSU in recent years, the Soviet side has made frequent breaches of the status quo on the border, occupied Chinese territory and provoked border incidents. Still more serious, the Soviet side has flagrantly carried out large-scale subversive activities in Chinese frontier areas, trying to sow discord among China's nationalities by means of the press and wireless, inciting China's minorities to break away from their motherland, inveigling and coercing tens of thousands of Chinese citizens into going into the Soviet Union.

> From a letter to the Chinese Central Committee from the Soviet Central Committee, 29 February 1964, quoted in the Chinese Press as above

(ii) In recent years, on her borders with neighbouring states, the Chinese side have been stooping to acts of a nature which gives us reason to think that the government of the People's Republic of China is departing on this question more and more from Leninist positions. Her leaders are deliberately concentrating the people's attention on frontier problems, artificially fanning nationalist passions and dislike for other peoples.

Since 1960, Chinese servicemen and civilians have been systematically violating the Soviet frontier. . . Attempts are also being made to 'develop' some parts of Soviet territory without permission. . .

The Soviet Government has already proposed many times to the Government of the People's Republic of China that consultations be held on the question of the demarcation of specific sections of the frontier line, so as to exclude any possibility of misunderstanding. However, the Chinese side evades such consultations, while at the same time continuing to violate the border.

> From a Soviet Government statement, 21 September 1963, quoted in *Pravda*

D The *People's Daily* on the Resignation of Khrushchev.

Khrushchev is the chief representative of modern revisionism. He has betrayed Leninism, proletarian internationalism, the path of the October Revolution and the interests of the Soviet people. The Soviet people and the CPSU recently removed him from leading posts in the Party and the State. This is a very good thing and it has the support of the Marxist-Leninists and the revolutionary people of the world. Facts have repeatedly borne out that the great wheel of history cannot be reversed by imperialism and the reactionaries, or by Khrushchev revisionism. Anyone who runs counter to Leninism . . . and the interests of the people will, sooner or later, be spurned by the people. This was so in the past, is so at present, and will be so in the future.

From a *People's Daily* editorial, 10 November 1965

E Sino-Soviet Views of the 'Brezhnev Doctrine', 1970

(i) The anti-socialist conspiracy in Czechoslovakia . . . was a long-premeditated attempt, prepared behind a screen of demagogy*, on the part of the remnants of the former exploiting classes, in alliance with right-wing opportunists and with the support of world imperialism, to destroy the foundations of the socialist system in Czechoslovakia, to isolate her from the fraternal countries, and thereby to strike a heavy blow against the position of socialism in Europe. But the staunchness of the Marxist-Leninist core of the Czechoslovak Communist Party and the determined action by Czechs and Slovaks devoted to the cause of socialism and by allied countries loyal to the principles of socialist internationalism frustrated the dangerous enemy plans directed against the common interests of socialism and, in the long run, against peace on the continent of Europe. . .

As for the Soviet Union, we take a resolute stand in favour of socialist internationalism and the restoration of good relations between socialist countries wherever they have been broken. We shall not be found wanting. The Central Committee of the CPSU and the Soviet Government will continue to work actively and consistently in this direction.

L.I. Brezhnev, at the Lenin Centenary Celebrations in the Kremlin, 21–22 April 1970

* demagogy = mob-rule

(ii) Since Brezhnev came to power, with its baton becoming less and less effective and its difficulties at home and abroad growing more and more serious, the Soviet revisionist renegade clique has been practising social imperialism and social-Fascism more frantically than ever. Internally it has intensified its suppression of the Soviet people and speeded up the all-round restoration of capitalism. Externally it has stepped up its collusion with US imperialism and its suppression of the revolutionary struggles of the people of various countries, intensified its control over and its exploitation of the various east European countries and the People's Republic of Mongolia . . . and intensified its threat of aggression against China. Its dispatch of hundreds of thousands of troops to occupy Czechoslovakia, and its armed provocations against

China on our territory are two foul performances staged recently by Soviet revisionism.

In order to justify its aggression and plunder, the Soviet revisionist renegade clique trumpets its so-called theory of 'limited sovereignty' and the theory of 'socialist community'. What does all this stuff mean? It means that your sovereignty is 'limited', while his is unlimited. You won't obey him? He will exercise his 'international dictatorship' over you – dictatorship over the people of other countries, in order to form the 'socialist community' ruled over by the new Tsars.

Marshal Lin, speaking at the 9th Party Congress of the CCP in Beijing,
1 April 1969

Questions

1 Use your own knowledge to explain the meaning of the phrase 'a cult of the personality'. Use Source A parts (i) and (ii) to show why this cult produced a rift between the USSR and Communist China after 1956. **(4 marks)**

2 Refer to Source B parts (i) and (ii) to show how the rift between the USSR and Communist China widened at the time of the Bucharest Conference in 1960. **(4 marks)**

3 Show how, according to Source C parts (i) and (ii), Sino-Soviet relations in the 1960s suffered as the result of border disputes. **(4 marks)**

4 Use Source D to illustrate the disapproval felt by the Chinese Communist leadership for Soviet 'revisionism'. **(5 marks)**

5 Use Source E parts (i) and (ii) to show how the Brezhnev Doctrine arose out of a perceived need for solidarity, but finished by arousing suspicions of interventionism. **(5 marks)**

6 How might all the Sources A–E be used to illustrate the importance in an authoritarian state of the media in the process of moulding public opinion? **(8 marks)**

12 THE COLD WAR TRIANGLE

Even while he was quarrelling so violently with the Soviet government, Mao kept up a campaign of propaganda against the West. Following independently-organized bomb tests, he exploded China's first nuclear device at Lop Nor in 1964, and threatened that in the event of an all-out nuclear war between China and the capitalist world it would be the West that was annihilated first, and the surviving Chinese would inherit the earth. As relations between the USA and the USSR improved, Chinese denunciations of both became more strident. From the tone of his propaganda, Mao seemed to suggest there was nothing to pick between his Russian and his American foes; the 'new Tsars' and the 'capitalist exploiters' were both the same under the skin.

It seemed therefore remarkable that in 1971 both Washington and Beijing underwent a change of heart. For one thing, President Nixon, always stronger on pragmatic issues than he was on ideological ones, declared his wish to deal with eastern Asia as it was, and not as US world theorists wished it to be; and as a result for the first time he faced the possibility of ditching the Nationalist regime of Jiang Jieshi in Formosa and coming to terms with China's real rulers in Beijing. He remained deeply involved in the Vietnam war, and was not averse to wooing the Chinese Communists and so driving a wedge between them and their allies in Hanoi. Behind Nixon's thinking lurked the realization that the USA could no longer successfully 'contain' China, as Dulles had wished to do, and that it was therefore necessary to come to terms with it. On the Chinese part, there was the simultaneous realization that a deal with the Americans would end the diplomatic isolation into which the country had been forced by a combination of US hostility, exclusion from the UN and more recently the quarrel with the Soviet Union. Little as this might square with the line their propaganda had been following, they too placed pragmatism before ideology.

Restrictions on trade and travel between the two countries were relaxed in 1971, and in response American and British table tennis teams were allowed to visit China in April – where they were promptly trounced by the Chinese experts at the game; but this *ping-pong diplomacy* (as it swiftly became known) achieved its ends in July when the US Secretary of State Dr Henry Kissinger visited Beijing, followed in February 1972 by President Nixon himself. In the meantime the USA abandoned its obstruction in the United Nations and admitted China to membership, so that now it gained a place in the General Assembly, and a permanent seat on the Security Council instead of Taiwan. In 1973 the USA negotiated an armistice in Vietnam, followed by an American withdrawal from the country. In 1975 the cordiality of the new Washington-Beijing axis was further improved by the death of Jiang Jieshi.

The Soviet reaction to these moves showed some uncertainty. The Russians applauded the admission of Communist China to the General Assembly of the UN, and to the Security Council, where it decisively tilted the balance of power in favour of the eastern bloc; but they were less sure on other matters. Brezhnev saw it as a threat of an unholy alliance between the USA and China against the interests of the Soviet Union, whilst others saw it more as a Chinese attempt to discourage the growth of friendly Soviet-US relations, and to check the peace process by hampering disarmament.

Sino-Soviet relations thus remained cool in spite of cautious efforts to improve them. By the mid-1970s it was clear that the familiar bilateral confrontation between the communist and non-communist worlds had disappeared, perhaps for ever. In its place there was now a triangle of power between Moscow, Beijing and Washington.

A President Nixon Heralds a New Attitude towards China

The 22-year hostility between ourselves and the People's Republic of China is . . . serious indeed in view of the fact that it determines our relationship with 750m talented and energetic people. It is a truism that an international order cannot be secure if one of the major powers remains largely outside it and hostile towards it. In this decade, therefore, there will be no more important challenge than that of drawing the People's Republic of China into a constructive relationship with the world community.

We recognize that China's long historical experience weighs heavily on contemporary Chinese foreign policy. China has had little experience of conducting diplomacy based on the sovereign equality of nations. For centuries China dominated its neighbours, culturally and politically. In the last 150 years it has been subjected to massive foreign interventions. Thus, China's attitude toward foreign countries retains elements of aloofness, suspicion and hostility. Under Communism these historical attitudes have been sharpened by doctrines of violence and revolution, proclaimed more often than followed as principles in foreign relations.

Another factor determining Communist Chinese conduct is the intense and dangerous conflict with the USSR. It has its roots in the historical development of the vast border areas between the two countries. It is aggravated by contemporary ideological hostility, by power rivalry and nationalist ambitions.

A clash between these two great powers is inconsistent with the kind of stable Asian structure we seek. We therefore see no advantage to us in the hostility between the Soviet Union and Communist China. We do not seek any. We will do nothing to sharpen that conflict – nor to encourage it. . .

We are prepared to establish a dialogue with Beijing. We cannot accept its ideological precepts, or the notion that Communist China must exercise hegemony over Asia. But neither do we wish to impose on China an international position that denies its legitimate national interests.

> From a Report to Congress on US Foreign Policy by President Nixon,
> 25 February 1971

B Sino-US Relations, 1971–72

(i) In October 1969 President Nixon said, with regard to Latin America, that 'we must deal realistically with Governments . . . as they are.' Both in Asia and elsewhere in the world we are seeking to accommodate our role to the realities of the world today. Our objective is to contribute, in practical terms, to the building of a framework for a stable peace.

No question of Asian policy has so perplexed the world in the last 20 years as the China question, and the related question of its representation in the United Nations. Basic to that question is the fact that each of the two Governments claims to be the sole Government of China and representative of all the people of China.

Representation . . . would provide Governments with increased opportunities for contact and communication. It would also help promote co-operation on common problems which affect all of the member-nations regardless of political differences.

The United States accordingly will support action at the General Assembly this fall calling for the seating of the People's Republic of China. At the same time the United States will oppose any action to expel the Republic of China* or otherwise deprive it of representation in the United Nations. . .

Our consultations have shown that any action to deprive the Republic of China of its representation would meet with strong opposition in the General Assembly. Certainly, as I have said, the United States will oppose it.

> Press Conference by Secretary of State William Rogers, 2 August 1971

* i.e. the Nationalist Government then resident in Taiwan

(ii) The American people are a great people. The Chinese people are a great people. The peoples of our two countries have always been friendly to each other but, owing to reasons known to all, the contacts between the two peoples were suspended for more than 20 years. Now, through the common effort of China and the United States, the gates to friendly contact have finally opened.

At the present time there is a strong desire on the part of the Chinese and the American people to work for the relaxation of tensions. The people and the people alone are the most important motive force in making world history, and the day will come when this common desire of our two peoples will be realized.

The social systems of China and the United States are fundamentally different, and there are great differences between the two Governments. However, these differences should not hinder China and the United States from establishing normal relations on the basis of the five principles: of mutual respect for the sovereignty and territorial integrity of nations; of mutual non-aggression; of non-interference in internal affairs; of mutual equality; and of peaceful co-existence.

Premier Zhou Enlai, welcoming President Nixon to Beijing, 21 February 1972

C Soviet Reactions to the Sino-American Rapprochement

(i) The representative of the USSR said that, ever since the inception of the People's Republic of China in 1949, the Soviet Union had consistently spoken out for the restoration of its rights in the United Nations and had refused to recognize the Jiang Jieshi delegation. His delegation had always stressed that China must be represented in the Organization by the representatives of the People's Republic of China. The policy of the United States and some of its allies had, for two decades, blocked the possibility of restoring the lawful rights of the People's Republic of China, but that policy and the policy of maintaining the Jiang Jieshi clique in the Organization had utterly failed. Life itself had confirmed the far-sighted policy of the Soviet Communist Party and the Soviet Government, which had consistently defended the principle of universality in the United Nations. That policy had made it possible to overcome the obstruction of imperialism. . . In welcoming the Chinese delegation, the representative of the USSR expressed the hope that the restoration of the rights of the People's Republic of China would bring about a positive contribution to the work of the United Nations to increase its effectiveness and strengthen mutual understanding and co-operation among peoples.

Report of the Soviet delegate, J.A. Malik, addressing the UN General Assembly, 25 October 1971

(ii) The participants in the Beijing meetings told their peoples and the world little about the content of their talks and the substance of the agreement reached by them. More than that, they intimated that it had been decided to keep it secret and not to discuss everything transcending this published official communiqué. Therefore, facts, the subsequent deeds of the United States and the PRC will say the decisive word about the significance of the Beijing talks. It is impossible, however, to overlook some statements of the participants of the Beijing talks that make one think that the dialogue goes beyond the framework of the bilateral relations between the United States and China. For instance, how else can one assess the statement made at a banquet in Shanghai that 'today our two peoples hold in their hand the future of the whole world'?

L.I. Brezhnev, quoted in *Pravda*, 21 March 1972

(iii) The Maoists' basic foreign policy has consisted and consists in preventing the implementation of the peace programme advanced by the 24th CPSU Conference, and, in particular, in preventing an improvement in Soviet-US relations. And if Beijing has proved not to possess sufficiently weighty arguments to prevent the constructive development of relations between our country and the United States, this, together with everything else, means that influential circles in Washington realize the objective difference between the great-power status with which they would have liked to invest Beijing, with a view to pursuing a variation of 'three-cornered diplomacy' advantageous to themselves, and the present real potential of Maoist foreign policy.

V.P. Lukin, in *Problems of Philosophy*, February 1973

Questions

1 What factors, according to Source A, stood in the way of an effective Chinese foreign policy in 1971, and to what extent was President Nixon prepared to encourage the development of more friendly Sino-US relations? **(6 marks)**

2 What support is indicated in Source B parts (i) and (ii) for improved Sino-US relations, and what limits do they suggest on this improvement? **(6 marks)**

3 Use Source C part (i), and your own knowledge, to contrast the attitude of the Soviet Union towards the People's Republic of China and the Nationalist regime in Taiwan. **(4 marks)**

4 Use Source C parts (ii) and (iii) to explain the suspicions with which the Soviet Union regarded any improvement in Sino-US relations. **(6 marks)**

5 'No great realignment.' What evidence is contained in all of the Sources A–C that the changes in the relations between the USA and the PRC in 1971 were less fundamental than is sometimes supposed? **(8 marks)**

13 DÉTENTE AND DISARMAMENT

In the wake of the Cuba crisis, in an effort to avert imminent catastrophe, the USA and the USSR agreed the Nuclear Test Ban Treaty of 1963 and the Nuclear Non-Proliferation Treaty of 1968, both of which later gained wide acceptance. Absorbed at the time in Vietnam, the United States was disinclined to embark on other world involvements, whilst for its part the Soviet Union under Brezhnev, though paying lip-service to hard-line policies, continued to pursue a moderate accommodation with the USA, much to the annoyance of the Chinese Communists. President Nixon, who made successive visits to Beijing and to Moscow in the early 1970s, and his Secretary of State Kissinger further improved relations between East and West. During their visit to Moscow in May 1972 two important agreements were signed as the result of the Strategic Arms Limitation Talks (or SALT). The first related to anti-ballistic missile systems (ABMs) and restricted the areas where such systems could be deployed; the other restricted the total numbers of inter-continental ballistic missiles (ICBMs) and submarine-launched ballistic missiles (SLBMs) that the two powers could continue to hold. Brezhnev continued the trend by visiting the United States in June 1973, where a second summit was held.

The improvement in relations, however, was not sustained. From the start there had been some Soviet unease over the terms of the new agreements, partly because they did not take into account the new American development of the multiple independently-targeted re-entry vehicle (MIRV) which threatened to shower a wide spread of targets with separately guided warheads from the same missile. Soon afterward, too, there occurred the Yom Kippur War, where both sides, though officially neutral, continued to supply their traditional allies with arms; Brezhnev indeed even threatened the Israelis with attack unless they respected the cease-fire called for by the Security Council.

Nevertheless their common interests continued to draw the two countries together. Nixon visited the USSR again in 1974 and further treaties were initialled: one banned underground weapons tests in excess of 150 kilotons; and another agreed to deploy only one ABM system. Further agreements related to new limitations on strategic arms, and to their intention to conclude a Conference on Security and Co-operation in Europe (CSCE). The former was settled by President Ford at a meeting with Brezhnev in Vladivostok in 1974; the latter produced the Helsinki Conference of 1975, whose Final Act covered European frontiers, human rights, disarmament, economic and scientific co-operation and a wide variety of linked issues.

However, the hopes of the mid-1970s were never realized. For one thing, Brezhnev was under increasing pressure from conservative communists to take a firmer stand against the capitalist West; for another, the Soviet Union, by a tremendous effort, had managed to achieve a near-equivalence with the United States in nuclear weaponry. The USA, for its part, had now freed itself from the obsession of Vietnam and felt more capable of action elsewhere. At the same time, voices were being raised in the United States against *détente*; even the new President, Jimmy Carter, with his life-long commitment to the question of human rights, was less inclined to be patient with a regime which he saw as the main enemy of these rights. As a result US military spending, including that for the benefit of America's allies – some of whom, like Iran under the Shah, had human rights records scarcely better than Brezhnev's – increased from about $45 billion in 1976 to $70 billion in 1979. The conclusion of SALT 2 in Vienna in June 1979, in the light of this spending, was little more than an empty gesture.

US-Soviet relations became even worse as the result of the Russian invasion of Afghanistan in 1979, and of signs of what was regarded as 'adventurism' in parts of Africa. This was partly in support of Cuban involvement in Angola and Zaire and partly on Russia's own account in the Sudan, Somalia and Mozambique. The incoming Reagan Administration in 1981 was thus much less inclined to bargain with the USSR, but instead persisted in regarding the Soviets as the 'forces of darkness'; one of its first acts was to reject the SALT 2 treaty when it came before the Senate for ratification.

The pattern of Reagan's thinking was therefore firmly set at the beginning of the 1980s, and was later extended to Latin America, where Reagan showed clear sympathy for right-wing elements in Grenada, Nicaragua and El Salvador. Not even the death of Brezhnev in 1982, and the eventual succession to power of reformist elements under Mikhail Gorbachev in 1985, altered US attitudes much. Reagan remained very suspicious of him until the end of his second term in 1988; even the incoming Bush Administration took time to come to terms with him.

However, by 1991 it seemed that old-style Marxist communism was breaking down. With it, the Soviet 'empire' in eastern Europe rapidly began to crumble, and Soviet provinces such as Armenia, the Ukraine and the Baltic states were demanding freedom from central control. Even the old party elite at the head of the system was disintegrating. Taken all together, the 'threat from the east' was no longer as frightening as it had been in former years.

A Khrushchev in London, April 1956

I remember one incident that captures the atmosphere of our talks in London. Bulganin, Lloyd* and I were riding in the same car on our way to visit some educational institution. Lloyd was very proper and friendly. At one point he turned to me and said 'You know, a little birdie perched on my shoulder the other day and chirped into my ear that you are selling arms to Yemen.'

I said 'Well, apparently there are all sorts of little birds flying about these days, chirping all kinds of different things, because one perched on my shoulder, too, and told me you're selling arms to Egypt and Iraq. This little birdie told me that you'll try to sell arms to anyone who will buy them from you and sometimes even to people who don't want to buy them from you.'

'I guess it's true: there are all sorts of birdies. Some of them are chirping in your ear, and some in ours.'

'Yes', I said, 'but wouldn't it be nice if all the little birdies started chirping the same thing in both of our ears – that we should assume a mutually binding obligation not to sell arms to anyone? Then wouldn't all the birdies be making a contribution to the common cause of peace?'

N.S. Khrushchev, in *Khrushchev Remembers*, ed. E. Crankshaw, 1971

* Selwyn Lloyd, then British Foreign Secretary under Sir Anthony Eden

B Two Views of the Test Ban Treaty, 1963

(i) This is a treaty signed by three nuclear powers. By this treaty they attempt to consolidate their nuclear monopoly and bind the hands of all the peace-loving countries subjected to the nuclear threat. . .

The people of the world demand general disarmament and a complete ban on nuclear weapons; this treaty completely divorces the cessation of nuclear tests from the total prohibition of nuclear weapons, legalizes the continued manufacture, stock-piling and use of nuclear weapons by the three nuclear powers, and runs counter to disarmament. . .

This treaty actually strengthens the position of nuclear powers for blackmail and increases the danger of imperialism launching a nuclear war and a world war.

If this big fraud is not exposed, it can do even greater harm. It is unthinkable for the Chinese Government to be a party to this dirty fraud. The Chinese Government regards it as its unshirkable and sacred duty to thoroughly expose this fraud.

Chinese Government statement reported in the *People's Daily*, Beijing,
31 July 1963

(ii) The Government of the PRC claims that the conclusion of the treaty banning nuclear weapon tests leads to 'American imperialism gaining a military advantage' while the peace-loving countries, including China, lose the 'possibility of strengthening their defensive might'.

Strange logic, this! Even our enemies admit that it is the Soviet Union that has the most powerful nuclear weapons in the world today and the most advanced means for delivering them to any target.

This powerful rocket-nuclear shield ensures the security not only of the Soviet Union but of all the socialist countries, including the PRC, and is the bulwark of peace throughout the world.

Does the conclusion of a treaty banning tests alter the present balance of forces? No, it doesn't. The Soviet Government would never have agreed to the conclusion of such a treaty if it placed us in an unequal position, if it gave unilateral advantages to the other side.

Soviet Government answer reported in *Pravda*, 4 August 1963

C *Détente* and Disarmament at the Third Brezhnev-Nixon Summit, July 1974

[Both sides are] deeply convinced of the imperative necessity of making the process of improving US-Soviet relations irreversible. . . The two sides continue steadfastly to apply their joint efforts . . . in such important fields as: removing the danger of war, including particularly war involving nuclear and other mass-destruction weapons; limiting and eventually ending the arms race, having in mind as the ultimate objective the achievement of general and complete disarmament under appropriate international control; contributing to the elimination of sources of international tension and military conflict; strengthening and extending the process of relaxation of tensions throughout the world; developing broad, mutually beneficial co-operation in commercial and economic, scientific-technical and cultural fields. . .

Taking into consideration the relationship between the development of offensive and defensive types of strategic arms, and noting the successful implementation of the Treaty on the Limitation of Anti-Ballistic Missile Systems concluded between them in May 1972, both sides considered it desirable to adopt additional limitations on the deployment of such systems. . .

Having noted the historic significance of the treaty banning nuclear weapon tests in the atmosphere, in outer space and under water, concluded in Moscow in 1963, both sides expressed themselves in favour of making the cessation of nuclear weapon tests comprehensive.

Joint Soviet-American Communiqué after the Moscow Summit meeting, July 1974

73

D President Ford on *Détente*

First, *détente* is an evolutionary process, not a static condition. Many formidable challenges yet remain. Second, the success of the *détente* process depends on new behaviour patterns that give life to all our solemn declarations. . . The people of all Europe and, I assure you, the people of North America are thoroughly tired of having their hopes raised and then shattered by empty words and phrases. We had better say what we mean and mean what we say, or we will have the anger of our citizens to answer. . . Finally there must be an acceptance of mutual obligations. *Détente*, as I have often said, must be a two-way street. Tensions cannot be eased by one side alone. Both sides must want *détente* and work to achieve it. . .

Military stability in Europe has kept the peace. While maintaining that stability, it is now time to reduce substantially the high levels of military forces on both sides. Negotiations now under way in Vienna on mutual and balanced force reductions so far have not produced the results for which I had hoped. The United States stands ready to demonstrate flexibility in moving these negotiations forward, if others will do the same. . . The United States also intends to pursue vigorously a further agreement on strategic arms limitation with the Soviet Union. This remains a priority of American policy. General Secretary Brezhnev and I agreed last November in Vladivostok the essentials of a new accord limiting strategic offensive weapons for the next ten years. We are moving forward in our bilateral discussions here in Helsinki.

President G. Ford, speaking at the conclusion of the Helsinki Conference,
1 August 1975

E Gorbachev and Reagan at Reykjavik, 1986

A whole set of major measures was submitted to the talks. These measures, if accepted, would usher in a new era in the life of mankind – a nuclear-free era. Herein lies the essence of the radical change in the world situation, the possibility of which was obvious and realistic. The talk was no longer about limiting nuclear arms, as was the case with SALT 1, SALT 2 and other treaties, but about the elimination of nuclear weapons within a comparatively short period of time. . .

I must tell you, comrades, that the President's initial reaction was not entirely negative. He even said 'What you have just stated is reassuring.' But it did not escape our attention that our US interlocutors appeared to be somewhat confused. At the same time, immediate doubts and objections cropped up in their separate remarks. Straight away, the President and the Secretary of State started talking about divergencies and disagreement. In their words we clearly discerned the familiar old tones we had heard at the Geneva negotiations for many months: we were reminded of all sorts of sub-levels on strategic nuclear armaments, the 'interim proposal' on missiles in Europe . . . and many other things in the same vein.

In the afternoon, we met again. The President announced the stand that had been agreed during the break. As soon as he uttered the first phrase it became clear that they were offering us the same old moth-eaten trash (as I put it at the press conference) from which the Geneva talks were already choking. . .

It was becoming clear, comrades, that the US representatives had come to Reykjavik with nothing at all to offer. . . The US President was not ready to take any radical decisions on questions of principle, to meet the Soviet side half-way, so as to give real impetus to productive and encouraging negotiations. This is precisely what I had impressed upon the President in my letter. . .

The President sought to touch upon ideological issues as well in these discussions and in this way demonstrated, to put it mildly, total ignorance and an inability to understand the socialist world and what is happening there. . .

As far as nuclear testing is concerned, it was perfectly clear why the US side does not want to conduct serious talks on this issue. It would have preferred to carry these talks on endlessly and thus postpone a settlement. . . I said bluntly that I was having doubts about the honesty of the US position. How can an agreement on the elimination of nuclear arms be reached if the US continues to perfect these weapons? We were under the impression that SDI* was the main snag. If it could have been removed it would have been possible to reach an accord. . .

Our proposals were major, truly large-scale and clearly in the nature of a compromise. We made concessions. But we did not see even the slightest desire on the US side to respond in kind or to meet us half-way. . .

The scope of our partners' approach was not broad enough. They did not grasp the uniqueness of the moment, and ultimately they did not have enough courage, sense of responsibility or political resolve which are all so needed to settle key and pressing issues in world politics. They stuck to old positions which had already eroded with time and did not correspond to the realities of today.

President M.S. Gorbachev, in a speech on Soviet television,
14 October 1986

* SDI = the Strategic Defence Initiative, or 'Star Wars' proposal (a scheme named after a popular science fiction movie and designed to provide the USA with complete anti-nuclear protection through a foolproof automated system operating in space, to detect and pick off approaching nuclear devices before they could do any harm).

Questions

1 What degree of friendliness does Source A show existed between the British and the Soviet governments in 1956? **(3 marks)**

2 What light do Source B parts (i) and (ii) throw on the state of Sino-Soviet relations in the 1960s? **(4 marks)**

3 How far, according to Source C, had *détente* between the USA and the USSR progressed by 1974? **(3 marks)**

4 How optimistic does Source D show President Ford to be on the subject of international *détente* in 1975? **(3 marks)**

5 a) What does Source E reveal of President Gorbachev's personal feelings towards President Reagan at the Reykjavik meeting? **(3 marks)**
   b) What reasons does President Gorbachev give in Source E for his disappointment with the attitudes of the US government at this meeting? **(3 marks)**
   c) How reliable, in your opinion, is Source E as historical evidence? **(5 marks)**

6 Use Sources A–E, and your own knowledge, to show to what extent, in your opinion, the prospects for international understanding were better in the late 1980s than they had been in the mid-1950s. **(6 marks)**

14 BREZHNEV TO GORBACHEV

The later part of Brezhnev's lengthy administration as Chairman of the CPSU and ruler of the Soviet Union bore all the marks of atrophy and stagnation. Partly this was due to his ill-health, but the real causes lay deeper. From the beginning he had leaned towards the conservative right, whose grip on political power was deliberately consolidated by his reversal of Khrushchev's more liberal policies, and gradually the powerful *nomenklatura* of the Party tightened their grip over the country and made him increasingly their puppet. But, although the Soviet Union was a rich country, its economic and industrial backwardness, and the strains that were placed upon it by Brezhnev's massive programme of rearmament, imposed impossible burdens on the long-suffering Soviet people. Whilst paying for an increasingly costly scientific research programme, building all the nuclear missiles that were needed for equivalence with the USA and maintaining enormous armies within its own territories and those of its allies, the Soviet Union frequently went short of bread and had to go cap-in-hand to the United States to augment its meagre food supplies. It was not only the vast numbers of party officials battening on to the economy and the considerable privileges they extracted by virtue of their social position that undermined the economic viability of the communist system; more particularly it became increasingly obvious that the 'command economy' – if it had ever worked satisfactorily – was fast breaking down. But the *nomenklatura* were too deeply entrenched in Soviet society to do anything about it, or even to admit that there was anything wrong.

However, although Brezhnev was illiberal he was not as actively repressive as Stalin had been, and Soviet society found itself able to breathe rather more freely than it had during the 1930s. So, though they might struggle to preserve their dominance in the political system, the conservatives were unable to check the spread of opposition ideas, or to preserve their tenure of power for long after Brezhnev's death in 1982. The rule of the conservative 'hard-liners' continued during the brief *interregnum* of Yuri Andropov (1982–84), which was followed by another even more brief, that of Constantin Chernenko (1984–85). But in 1985 Mikhail Gorbachev succeeded as Chairman of the CPSU at the comparatively youthful age of 54, and a new spirit of reform swept through the Kremlin.

Glasnost (openness) and *perestroika* (restructuring) became the new catchwords. The Soviet Union was opened up to debate and criticism. But still suspicion remained of a state that ruled through arbitrary power. Gorbachev nevertheless started the process of reform, ignoring the pessimistic view of the conservatives that he was sawing off the branch on which he was sitting. It was the first of Gorbachev's many gambles, but it paid off. Liberals in Russia began to believe in change, and the world started to trust the Soviet leader and to believe he could deliver results. Soon the USA and the USSR, countries which had recently been glowering at each other, found themselves on a common path. The charismatic Chairman (soon to be President) Gorbachev soon outshone the former film-star Ronald Reagan. But the scale of the Soviet proposals at Reykjavik in 1986 stunned the Americans, and for a time they seemed unable to take them in. However Gorbachev knew that he had to slash military spending if he was to avoid bankruptcy. It took two more years of negotiation before the two were ready to sign the first major treaty, abolishing medium-range nuclear missiles. Soon Gorbachev ordered the Soviet withdrawal from Afghanistan, followed by the even more radical offer to withdraw his armies from eastern Europe. US inspectors were admitted to top-secret Soviet bases to witness the destruction of surplus missiles, whilst Soviet military men sat in on NATO meetings.

Gorbachev based his foreign policy not on class struggle, but on mutual benefit. The same was true of his dealings with China. This was the first, but by no means the last, piece of Marxist dogma which he jettisoned.

A The Later Policies of Chairman Brezhnev

The immediate pretext for the Soviet invasion of Afghanistan was the need to secure in power, following the so-called 'Brezhnev Doctrine', the client Marxist regime which had been established by a coup in 1978. Russia had recently signed a friendship and co-operation treaty with that regime, but now it faced opposition from Islamic tribal guerrillas. This client regime had provided the Russians with a useful military base within fighter plane reach of the oil states of the Middle East. A secondary consideration was the importance of securing Afghanistan as a reliable buffer state on Russia's southern borders and to prevent the spread of Islamic revivalism into Turkestan, an increasingly important demographic and economic region within the Soviet Union. . .

It is clear, however, that sanction for such an action would not have been forthcoming unless there had been important changes . . . in foreign policy perceptions which gave the upper hand to the more 'hawkish' groupings. Such changes did occur, with the voice of the military becoming much stronger within the Politburo and the key executive organs during the closing years of the 1970s. This military lobby favoured the use of Russia's new military muscle in pursuance of its foreign policy objectives. This view gained broader support among less hawkish policy makers as it became clear during the final months of 1979 that the US Senate – with a third of its members facing re-election in 1980 – was almost certain to dismember or reject the Salt 2 agreement, and that the 1980 Presidential elections would return a conservative Republican leader, Ronald Reagan...

The repercussions of the Afghanistan invasion proved, however, in hindsight to be even more far-reaching than Soviet leaders had anticipated. Firstly, victory in the military campaign against Afghan Mujaheddin rebels, supplied with Chinese and American arms, was not as quick and decisive as had been expected. Russian troops were able to gain control of urban centres, but were faced with guerrilla resistance in the countryside. Eight years later this guerrilla warfare had accounted for more than 50 000 Soviet casualties and was continuing to tie up more than 100 000 Soviet troops and impose a mounting economic burden on the Soviet regime. Secondly, the Afghanistan campaign lost Russia friends in the Islamic world, among the Third World and non-aligned community and contributed substantially to a further deterioration in relations with China, pushing the latter power closer to the United States. Thirdly, the Afghanistan invasion brought in its wake Western sanctions – a temporary US grain and high-technology export embargo and a partial Western boycott of the 1980 Moscow Olympics, followed by the collapse of the SALT 2 agreement and the start of a Western arms build-up. A US rapid-deployment force was set up to police the Persian Gulf; NATO defence ministers agreed to increase their military budgets by at least three per cent per annum (in real terms) between 1980 and 1986; and plans were made to deploy Pershing 2 and Cruise intermediate ballistic missiles (IBMs) in western Europe to counter Russian SS-20s. In the United States a new right-wing anti-Soviet President, Ronald Reagan, was elected in the winter of 1980 determined to build up American military strength...

[But] Brezhnev's period of personal dominance proved to be short-lived. Ailing personal health began to weaken the grip of a man who had been renowned, during the 1960s and early 1970s, particularly overseas, for his drive, energy and boisterousness. In 1975 and 1977 Brezhnev suffered two serious strokes and was forced to have a pace-maker fitted and undergo facial surgery. His speech became slurred, his movement shaky and he began to vanish for months on end to rest at treatment clinics in the Crimea... The final years of the Brezhnev administration thus became ones of party sclerosis and general drift.

Adapted from Ian Derbyshire, *The Soviet Union from Brezhnev to Gorbachev*, 1989

B Gorbachev on Social Progress

Will the ruling centres of the capitalist world manage to embark on the path of sober, constructive assessments of what is going on? The easiest thing is to say: maybe yes and maybe no. But history denies us the right to make such predictions. We cannot take 'no' for an answer to the question: will mankind survive or not? We say: the progress of society, the life of civilization, must and shall continue. . .

We are realists and are perfectly well aware that the two worlds are divided by very many things, and deeply divided, too. But we also see clearly that the need to resolve most vital problems affecting all humanity must prompt them to interaction, awakening humanity's heretofore unseen powers of self-preservation. . .

The course of history, of social progress, requires ever more insistently that there should be constructive and creative interaction between states and peoples. . .

The Communists have always been aware of the intrinsic complexity and contradictoriness of the paths of social progress. But at the centre of these processes – and this is the chief distinction of the Communist world outlook – there unfailingly stands man, his interests and cares. Human life, the possibilities for its comprehensive development, as Lenin stressed, is of the greatest value; the interests of social development rank above all else. That is what the CPSU takes its bearings from in its practical policy.

M.S. Gorbachev, from the Political Report of the CPSU Central Committee at the 27th Party Congress, 25 February 1986

C Gorbachev on Soviet Foreign Policy

We have talked a good deal about the process of reorganization in our country. I want to repeat in this context: our foreign policy today stems directly from our domestic policy to a larger extent than ever before.

We say honestly for all to hear: we need peace to concentrate on the development of our society and to tackle the tasks of improving the life of the people. . .

We hope that the in-depth dialogue we are conducting with Western countries and our positions and intentions, which we have been talking about frankly and backing up with practical action, as well as this visit of yours, esteemed Mrs Prime Minister, and our forthright talks, will finally form a subject for serious deliberation and invite reciprocal moves. . .

The world today is one in which a struggle is under way between reason and madness, morality and savagery, life and death. We have determined our place in this struggle definitely and irreversibly. We are on the side of reason, morality and life. This is why we are for disarmament, and for creating a system for general security. This is the only possible way in which mankind can regain immortality.

M.S. Gorbachev, in a speech at a banquet in the Kremlin in honour of Margaret Thatcher, British Prime Minister, 30 March 1987

D Gorbachev on Nuclear Weapons in Outer Space

Space must remain peaceful; strike weapons must not be deployed there. And there must also be introduced very strict control, including the opening of the relevant laboratories for inspection.

Mankind is at a crucial stage of the new space age. It is time to abandon the thinking of the stone age, when the chief concern was to have a bigger stick or a heavier stone. We are against weapons in space. Our material and intellectual capabilities make it possible for the Soviet Union to develop any weapon if we are compelled to do so. But we are fully aware of our responsibility to the present and future generations. It is our profound conviction that we should approach the third millenium not with the Star Wars* programme, but with large-scale projects of peaceful space exploration by all mankind. We propose to start practical work in developing and implementing such projects. This is one of the most important ways of ensuring progress on our entire planet and establishing a reliable system of security for all.

M.S. Gorbachev, in a Disarmament Proposal (to be pursued at the US-Soviet talks in Geneva), 15 January 1986

* See Unit 13 Source E and footnote

E Gorbachev on Soviet Policies towards Asia

First of all, in keeping with its principled policy as approved by the 27th Congress, the Soviet Union will try to invigorate its bilateral relations with all countries without exception. We shall strengthen in every way friendship and promote many-sided relations with the Mongolian People's Republic, the Democratic People's Republic of [North] Korea, the Socialist Republic of Vietnam, the Lao People's Democratic Republic and the People's Republic of Campuchea. At present, for instance, a question of withdrawing a substantial part of Soviet troops from Mongolia is being considered jointly by the Soviet and Mongolian leadership. . .

Speaking in a city which is but a step from the People's Republic of China, I would like to dwell on the most important issues in our relations. These relations are extremely important for several reasons, starting with the fact that we are neighbours, that we share the world's longest land border, and that for this reason alone we, our children and grandchildren, are destined to live near each other 'for ever and ever'.

Relations between our two countries have improved noticeably in recent years. I would like to reaffirm that the Soviet Union is prepared – at any time and at any level – to enter into discussion with China on additional measures for establishing an atmosphere of good-neighbourliness. . .

As far as it is possible to judge, the Soviet Union and China have similar priorities – to accelerate social and economic development. Why not support each other, why not cooperate in implementing our plans wherever this is clearly to the benefit of both sides? The better our relations, the more we shall be able to share our experience.

We note with satisfaction that a positive shift has become visible in economic ties. We are convinced that the historically established complementarity between the Soviet and the Chinese economies offers great opportunities for expanding these ties, especially in the border regions. For instance, we do not want the Amur, which runs along the Chinese-Soviet border, to be viewed as a 'water-barrier'. Let the basin of this mighty river unite the efforts of the Chinese and Soviet peoples in using the river's rich resources for mutual benefit. . .

The Soviet Government is preparing a positive reply concerning the question of assistance in building a railway connecting the Xinjiang-Uygur Autonomous Region with Kazakhstan.

We have suggested cooperation with China in space exploration, which could include the training of Chinese cosmonauts. The opportunities for mutually beneficial exchanges in the sphere of culture and education are great. We are prepared for and sincerely desire all this.

M.S. Gorbachev, in a speech at a meeting in Vladivostok to award the city the Order of Lenin, 28 July 1986

Questions

1 Use Source A, and your own knowledge, to explain:
   a) the reasons for the Soviet intervention in Afghanistan in 1979, and its consequences. **(4 marks)**
   b) the reasons why Soviet policies lost momentum in the last five years of Brezhnev's rule. **(3 marks)**

2 Use Sources B, C and D to provide instances of Gorbachev's:
   a) loyalty to communist teachings. **(4 marks)**
   b) practical realism and political originality. **(6 marks)**

3 What evidence is contained in Source E of Gorbachev's professed desire to end the Sino-Soviet dispute? **(5 marks)**

4 How far do Sources B–D go in explaining Gorbachev's popularity in the West? Refer in your answer to each of these three sources. **(8 marks)**

15 THE END OF THE COLD WAR

The end of the 1980s saw profound changes in the climate of opinion in eastern Europe. This was partly due to the reassurance the people there felt at the liberal inclinations of the new Soviet leadership under Gorbachev; but it was undoubtedly also due to their mounting dissatisfaction with communism. This had simmered under the surface for years, breaking out in popular insurrection from time to time, but generally was repressed through fear by the security authorities; but now it was growing more vociferous. In general it focused on low living standards, poor wages, chronic shortages and industrial inefficiency; but in particular it raged against mismanagement and the self-interest and privilege of the *nomenklatura* – that fortunate minority who seemed to be the main beneficiaries of the entire system. Many of these eastern European leaders reacted in the only way they knew how, by clamping down on the protest and tightening their control. Gorbachev's attitude, when he visited these countries, was one of mild encouragement for the reform process. There was no reason, he believed, why *glasnost* and *perestroika* should not be given a place amongst their policies, as it was in the USSR. Two results stemmed from these developments: east European peoples were emboldened in their criticisms and their demands, and the east European bureaucracies felt that the Soviet leader had pulled the rug from under them, and was denying them the backing they felt they deserved.

Cracks began to appear in the monolithic communist structures in eastern Europe, and discontent was soon bubbling up through them. In Poland, orderly change, however reluctantly, began to take place. In August 1989 power was handed to moderate reformers, and in 1990 the first free elections were held for over half a century. In East Germany, where Erich Honecker had for so long held out firmly against change, the demand for reform mounted until it became irresistible. Restrictions between East and West Germany were progressively relaxed during 1989; the Wall came down and the Iron Curtain was dismantled. Eventually Honecker was removed and the two Germanies were reunited. At the same time, democratic changes were undertaken in Czechoslovakia, in Hungary and elsewhere. In Romania, one of the most repressive communist regimes was bloodily overthrown and the previous dictator tried and summarily executed. As the dank fog of communism cleared, a new eastern Europe began to appear, the liberated forces of European nationalism now very powerful, and to some observers seeming almost as threatening as the old communist power-bloc.

Hence the Warsaw Pact was no longer feasible on the old terms, and the new governments began to pursue their own foreign policies. In place of the Brezhnev Doctrine, which prescribed intervention for the preservation of European communist regimes, more than one observer suggested that Europe was now witnessing the Sinatra Doctrine ('I did it my way').

The Soviet Union itself was not immune to the nationalist virus. Beginning with outlying provinces which had never been happy with their shotgun marriages with the USSR, such as the Baltic states and Georgia, and later extending into Belorussia and the Ukraine, provincial separatism grew more clamorous, and by the summer of 1991 was beginning to question the whole basis on which the Soviet Union was built. Half-hearted efforts were made by Gorbachev to discourage the nationalists, but in the main he, seeing the need for basic changes in his own country, was already more than halfway towards recognizing the justice of their claims. The KGB, the Soviet Army and the conservatives in the Kremlin grew steadily more alarmed, threatening the breakaway states with violence and intimidating them into submission. In August, an attempted right-wing coup against Gorbachev failed, not because of his own strength, but because of the stout resistance put up by Boris Yeltsin, the elected President of the Russian Federation, and the weakness of the plotters themselves. In the wake of this coup it appeared that the old USSR had all but disappeared, and that the constituent republics had to get down afresh to the task of hammering out new relationships between the states who wished to modernize the Union. The break-up of the old Union became a fact at the end of 1991.

A Free Presidential Elections in Poland, 1990

As widely expected, Lech Walesa, leader of the Solidarity trade union and the country's most prominent opposition figure, gained a majority of the vote in the first direct presidential elections held in Poland, on 25 November. The unexpected element in the result, however, was that second place went not to Prime Minister Tadeusz Mazowiecki but to Stanislaw Tyminski, an émigré businessman who had no previous political experience and was virtually unknown until the last weeks of the campaign.

Official results released on 27 November showed that Walesa had gained 39.96% of the vote, Tyminski 23.10% and Mazowiecki 18.08%; the other three candidates gained 18.86% between them. Since none of the candidates gained an overall majority, Walesa and Tyminski would contest a run-off for the Presidency on 9 December.

The elections had been called in early October after President Wojciech Jaruzelski, the last remaining communist head of state in eastern Europe except for Albania, had agreed to resign just over a year into his second six-year term and to transfer power to a freely elected head of state.

There was a relatively low turn-out of just over 60%. Analysts interpreted the outcome as indicative of widespread disenchantment with the reform programme of the Mazowiecki government, launched in January and the most far-reaching in eastern Europe to date, which had precipitated a sharp rise in unemployment and a fall in living standards. Another factor was thought to be disillusionment . . . with the internal rivalry between the two wings of Solidarity, as represented by Walesa and Mazowiecki.

While Walesa endorsed the government's reform programme in principle, he argued it should be accelerated to avert social unrest. He argued that he, as President, would be best placed to 'complete the task' of establishing a market economy and a democratic political system in Poland. He accused the government of not removing former communists from positions of power in industry and government.

In turn, Mazowiecki argued that the reforms should be continued at a cautious pace which would minimize damage to the social and economic framework. Reflecting the deep split within Solidarity, the Mazowiecki camp also accused Walesa of autocratic tendencies, contradictory demagogy and a lack of clear policies.

Emerging as the main beneficiary of the division within Solidarity, Tyminski had at first been considered a rank outsider and was thus largely ignored by the media and other candidates, but began to attract support with claims that he was untarnished by past politics, and that as a self-made millionaire he had the economic acumen to transform the Polish economy. . .

After calling an extraordinary Cabinet meeting as the extent of his defeat became clear, Mazowiecki announced the resignation of his government.

He declared on television that 'Poland's painful but necessary programme of getting out of economic catastrophe can only be realized with the understanding of the majority of the nation' and that 'the country had made its choice'. On 29 November Parliament decided that it would not debate the resignation, thus formally keeping the government in power, effectively in a caretaker capacity until the election of the new President.

News Report in *Keesings Contemporary Archives* for November 1990

B The Breaching of the Berlin Wall, 1989

The most powerful symbol of postwar German divisions, the
Brandenburg Gate, reopened yesterday after 28 years in the presence of
the leaders of both Germanies and thousands of cheering East and
West Berliners.

Crowds from both parts of the city flocked in the pouring rain to watch
Herr Helmut Kohl, the West German Chancellor, step into East Berlin for
the first time and shake hands with Herr Hans Modrow, the East
German Prime Minister.

Holding his hands high in a gesture of victory, the Chancellor said:
'This is one of the most important moments in my life. Standing here, I
feel that we are in Germany, and that we will do everything in our power
to achieve unity.'

The two wide gaps struck in the Wall behind the Gate on Thursday
night failed to accommodate the surge of crowds from both sides. West
Berliners scrambled over the Wall to meet their fellow-townspeople in
East Berlin underneath the portals of the Gate, while East German
border guards wearing flowers joined the crowd in toasting the opening
with champagne.

In an atmosphere reminiscent of the opening of the border on
November 9th, strangers hugged and kissed.

Herr Modrow said: 'The Brandenburg Gate crossing is not just one of
many . . . the burning stench of war must never again be smelled here. It
must be the gate of peace.'

Herr Walter Momper, the Mayor of West Berlin, told the crowd: 'Life
in our city is now normal again.' Many shouted: 'We are one people!'
and waved West German flags, confirming the old adage that the winds
of history always blow first through the Brandenburg Gate.

News article in *The Times*, 23 December 1989

C The Downfall of the Ceausescu Regime in Romania, 1989

The Ceausescu regime was widely condemned for corruption and for
economic mismanagement, which left the vast majority of Romanians
with insufficient food and power. The rural systematization programme
had further alienated many of the country's villagers. It was widely
agreed that Ceausescu had remained in power only due to his powerful
and repressive internal security apparatus, centred around the
Securitate police.

The immediate trigger for the unrest which culminated in the
revolution was the deportation order served on 15 December on Fr
Laszlo Tokes, a Protestant pastor who had persistently criticized the

Government's treatment of his fellow ethnic Hungarians in Romania.

On 16 December several hundred people surrounded Fr Tokes's home in the western city of Timisoara, in an effort to prevent the police putting the deportation order into effect. The crowd . . . was joined by others in a march through the centre of Timisoara chanting 'Down with Ceausescu!' and 'Give us bread!' Further protests took place in the town on 17 December. Securitate police and troops, some in tanks or helicopter gunships, opened fire; several hundred people were reportedly killed. . .

Despite the killings the demonstrations grew in magnitude over the following days, spreading to other parts of the country. Troops in Timisoara withdrew from the streets on 20 December after workers had occupied and threatened to blow up a petrochemical plant. After a demonstrating crowd of over 50 000 people had attacked Communist Party and police offices, the Mayor of Timisoara invited the people to elect a committee to voice their grievances. . .

Returning on 20 December from a three-day visit to Iran, Ceausescu made a broadcast speech that evening, declaring a state of emergency in Timisoara and blaming 'terrorists, fascists, imperialists, hooligans and foreign espionage services' for the disturbances.

On 21 December Ceausescu addressed a large rally in central Bucharest. . . His speech, to his evident astonishment, was interrupted by unprecedented heckling, leading to scuffles between members of the crowd and Securitate men. . . In the morning of 22 December, while huge crowds gathered in Bucharest to protest against the regime, Ceausescu declared a national state of emergency. . .

Ceausescu made a final attempt a few hours later to address the hostile crowd from the balcony of the Communist Party central committee building, but was shouted down with cries of 'Death! Death!' Shortly after he finished speaking, demonstrators broke into the building. Apparently under orders from their commanders, troops made no attempt to intervene. Shortly after 1 pm local time, Ceausescu and his wife, accompanied by bodyguards, were airlifted by helicopter from the roof, even as the demonstrators emerged on to it. . . By the end of 22 December the revolutionaries in Bucharest had to some extent organized themselves into the National Salvation Front (NSF) with its headquarters in the television station. . .

At the height of the fighting, on 23 December, the NSF appealed to the Soviet Union to intervene militarily on its behalf. A Soviet spokesman said the following day that Moscow would only intervene if the revolution was under attack from foreign forces. Both the US and the Soviet governments, together with most of those of the rest of Europe, East and West, declared open support for the revolution.

Nicholae and Elena Ceausescu were captured on 22 December near Tirgoviste, 80km north-west of Bucharest. They had abandoned their helicopter near the Boteni air base, commandeering a car which subsequently broke down, and travelling on in a second car to a nearby agricultural station, where they were swiftly arrested and held under close guard in an armoured car. They were placed on trial before a military tribunal at a barracks near Tirgoviste on 25 December. Facing a range of charges including genocide, corruption and the destruction of the national economy, they were both condemned to death and executed by firing squad. Televised excerpts of the trial, and pictures of their corpses, were broadcast on Romanian television the following day.

News Report of events in Romania in *Keesings Contemporary Archives*, December 1989

D The Ending of the Warsaw Pact, 1991

At a meeting of the political and consultative committee of the Warsaw Treaty Organization in Budapest on 25 February, foreign and defence ministers from Bulgaria, Czechoslovakia, Hungary, Poland, Romania and the Soviet Union unanimously approved and signed a protocol cancelling the validity of all military agreements, organs and structures of the Warsaw Treaty with effect from 31 March.

Moves to dissolve the military alliance, which were first apparent at a Warsaw Pact summit meeting in June 1990, were intensified after January 1991. They were followed by reports on 11 February that the Soviet President Mikhail Gorbachev had written to leaders of member states recommending 'the liquidation of Warsaw Pact military structures by 1 April.'. . .

A communiqué issued after the 25 February meeting said that the decision to dismantle the Treaty's military organization had been taken by 'member states . . . acting as sovereign states with equal rights'. It noted that the 'elimination of Europe's dividedness offers a historical possibility to attain a new quality in security relations' based on each state's 'freedom of choice'.

At a press conference attended by participants from all member states except the Soviet Union, Hungarian Foreign Minister Geza Jeszensky revealed that members had held 'different views' concerning the Treaty's political structures, which ministers had agreed to transform temporarily into a purely voluntary consultative organization. It was understood that while ministers from eastern European member states had been keen to dissolve the entire organization, preferably by the end of 1991, the Soviet delegation had expressed a preference for the continuation of a bloc as a counterpart to NATO, at least until the conclusion of the talks related to the Helsinki process.

News Report in *Keesings Contemporary Archives*, February 1991

E The Process of Change in the Soviet Union, 1991

Mother Russia has finally resolved to settle the family's bitter feuds, open her arms wide and welcome back her lost children. . .

In the most ambitious of several competing plans, up to 800 more or less distinguished émigrés are expected to descend on Moscow shortly for a grandly named Congress of Compatriots. They will attend services in places such as the Kremlin's Cathedral of the Dormition and the Novodevichy monastery, which have been silent for most of the last 74 years.

They will also join senior academics, writers and officials in worthy discussions on Russia's heritage. And times being what they are, they will inevitably be guided towards Russia's new class of business managers and entrepreneurs and asked if they can see their way to a little investment.

The 12-day exercise will also feature events in Leningrad and Sverdlovsk (St Petersburg and Yekaterinburg, to use their past, and probably future, names) as well as two less romantic cities, Perm and Novosibirsk. The plan is supported by Boris Yeltsin, clearly counting on his new-found legitimacy as a popularly-elected, non-communist leader of Russia.

Article in *The Times*, 14 August 1991

F The Russian Tricolour Flies Again, 1991

None of us imagined it could happen so soon or so triumphantly: the raising – to rapturous clapping from hundreds of thousands of people – of the red, white and blue flag of pre-revolutionary Russia over the battered white building now vying with the Kremlin as Moscow's seat of political power.

The hauling down over the Russian parliament of the old communist banner, and its replacement by the tricolour, was the culmination of a vast, triumphant rally at which the new heroes of Russian democracy – Boris Yeltsin, Eduard Shevardnadze, and the Mayor of Moscow, Gavriil Popov – soared to new heights of moral authority.

Previous attempts to reintroduce the pre-1917 flag have been voted down by the Communists, but the political climate has suddenly changed and moves which seemed outrageous sacrilege a week ago seem unavoidable now.

The rally was an outpouring of joy, gratitude and relief by people who had seen the scotching of a monster that had threatened to blight each of their lives.

The monster's ghastly reappearance had suddenly made people count blessings – freedom to read books and decent newspapers, freedom to travel, freedom to pursue happiness in a dozen ways never conceived by an intrusive state – that many had ceased consciously to notice...

With almost perfect discipline and good manners, they started walking to the Kremlin; but because the weather was so good the mood was joyful, more of a stroll than a march.

They poured into the august square, past Lenin's tomb and the Kremlin walls, occupying a space still considered too sacred for any demonstrations but the rallies of May Day and Revolution Day. A rather embarrassed young man in a neat suit and tie had tried through a megaphone to guide them in an orderly walk round the Kremlin and lead them in chants of 'Yeltsin' and 'Russia'. It was at this point that events became almost surreal; one group of demonstrators was standing outside the steel-grey building that houses the Central Committee headquarters chanting 'Down with the Communists!' with joyful impunity and emitting piercing wolf whistles.

If all this sounds like ill-bred hooliganism, it was nothing of the kind – in the circumstances and by the standards of Russian public manners, the crowd's behaviour was a study in restraint. But one group tied ropes and chains round the statue of Felix Dzerzhinsky, the Pole who is notorious as the father of the Soviet secret police, and tried to tear it down. A tricolour was planted impishly above the communist building's door.

News Report in *The Times*, 23 August 1991

Questions

1 What evidence is there in Source A to show that political democracy was returning to Poland by the end of 1990? **(3 marks)**

2 What does Source B reveal of the feelings of many Germans about the breaching of the Berlin Wall in 1989? **(3 marks)**

3 Use Sources A, B and C, and your own knowledge, to contrast the different ways in which communist regimes came to an end in eastern Europe, 1989–90. **(6 marks)**

4 What evidence is there in Source D of the different attitudes of many of the parties involved towards the dissolution of the Warsaw Pact in 1991? **(4 marks)**

5 Use Sources E and F, and your own knowledge, to show how radical were the changes taking place in the Soviet Union in the summer of 1991. **(6 marks)**

6 Use all the Sources A–F to illustrate the importance to the historian of secondary historical sources. **(8 marks)**

16 PROPAGANDA PRESENTATION OF THE COLD WAR

Not surprisingly, the tone of most Cold War cartoons is unashamedly partisan. Those originating east of the Iron Curtain take the line dictated by the political establishment; in a country like the Soviet Union, with only very limited freedom of the press, it is unusual for publications to express anti-government opinions. However, Western publications reflect a much wider variety of opinion; a number do reflect the policies and attitudes of the government, but others question these, or else express views directly hostile to them.

'Good' cartoons are generally those which provide the public with witty and succinct comment on current issues. A gifted cartoonist, whilst expressing thoughts that are his own, has the ability to reflect in his work thoughts which were not far from the surface of the minds of many others. It is this which explains the cartoon's popularity.

In the case of the Soviet media, cartoons seem to express the opinions which the ruling group wish to propagate; a hostile observer might accuse them of forming part of the conditioning process to which nearly all authoritarian regimes subject their peoples. In fact the truth is more complex – and less dissimilar from what happens in the West than would at first appear. At a given time there are only a limited number of issues under discussion, and the differences between the views conveyed is often one of style rather than one of content. Furthermore, the ideological slant of a cartoon is not only conditioned by the prevalent modes of political thought, but because of the degree of simplification involved in this type of art the slant is frequently quite close to the surface. Hence the uniformity of approach which seems to be evident in many cartoons, and hence, too, the curious fact that those in the West may find, in spite of the language barrier, that Soviet cartoons are almost as easy to understand as their own.

Cartoons from East and West reflect issues central to the time from which they originate: matters to do with current international crises, with disarmament proposals then under discussion, with social and political comments on regimes of which the cartoonist either approves or disapproves. They may reflect criticisms being made of policy initiatives currently under way by the leaders of the other side, in a number of cases in the West, for example, criticisms of policies by the leaders of their own side.

A A Peep under the Iron Curtain

B The Bear Trainer

C 'Kept in after School' – Israel, France and Britain endure their
   Punishment

D Kennedy Under Pressure

E 'Captain Brezhnev Runs Aground' – Russia under Brezhnev's Command

F 'This Way to Destruction – The NATO Traffic Cop'. The signpost in this cartoon reads 'To Western Europe'; the letters on the baton read 'NATO'

G John Bull in His Lion Skin – 'Will you take this for cash?' The sign
over the kiosk reads 'International Finance Funds'

H **Land of the Free. The captions on the seven shadows behind the Statue of Liberty read: 'Discrimination', 'Police Terror', 'Crisis', 'Unemployment', 'Crime', 'Destitution'**

Questions

1 Study Source A, and explain:
   a) The message of the cartoon, and **(3 marks)**
   b) Why this message seemed appropriate at the time the cartoon was published (you may refer in your answer if you wish to Unit 1 Source B). **(3 marks)**

2 Which of the cartoons relates to the Cuban Missiles Crisis? Interpret the message of the cartoon, explaining whether it was friendly or hostile to the United States government. **(5 marks)**

3 Which of the cartoons expresses amusement and contempt for Britain? How does the cartoon convey these feelings, and what international events in the post-war world gave rise to them? **(6 marks)**

4 Study Sources B, E and H and explain:
   a) The message of each cartoon, and
   b) How accurately it reflected the public thinking of the country in which it originated. **(3 × 6 marks)**

5 Use as many of Sources A–H as you wish to assess the value of political cartoons as historical evidence. **(5 marks)**

17 THE HISTORIOGRAPHY OF THE COLD WAR

No historical account is absolutely unbiased, and this includes accounts of the Cold War. The most virulent form of bias comes about when a writer holds to an opinion in the face of all the evidence, on account of the prejudices with which the subject is approached. Thus it is possible for different writers, even using the same evidence, to come to quite different conclusions about the subjects under discussion. In these circumstances, one account is *not* as good as another. The less reliable authors of these accounts may be unaware of evidence which is contrary to their preconceived attitudes; but when, knowing of this evidence, they suppress it, they are guilty of deliberate dishonesty. The honest ones will seek to revise their conclusions in the light of the evidence that is newly come to hand. Unfortunately, historical evidence is sometimes so confusing and contradictory that the writer may not actually *know* the direction in which it is pointing.

This latter case applies to the Cold War. A number of writers, casting themselves in the role of spokesperson for their countries or their governments, do not search too hard for evidence which conflicts with their preconceptions, but present their conclusions in the clear-cut way that these dictate; any discrepancies do not worry them unduly. Those whose doubts have been roused will often probe more deeply, and reach different conclusions. Sometimes the views put forward by different writers are so contradictory that it is difficult to say, without further elaborate research, which is the correct interpretation; and where this is not possible, the matter has to be decided on the balance of probabilities. This is what is meant by the oft-quoted saying that good historians can be distinguished by the excellency of their guesswork.

Students may perhaps be guided best by taking the situation of the author into account when assessing the value of what has been written. A *contemporary* author may not adequately assess the importance for the future of the events under discussion, which may be played down, or thought more important than they turn out to be. If an author is perceptive, or writing with all the benefit of hindsight, they may be much closer to the target. Likewise an author with a vested interest – perhaps a career interest, say in the armed forces, or politics, or the diplomatic service (or even in journalism) – is less to be trusted than the more independent investigator who is trying to uncover the truth. This is even the case when their *position of privilege* (i.e. being in a situation in which they have access to the facts) entitles them to be believed, for there may be powerful forces combining to subvert their judgement.

A The Position of the Powers Post-war

(i) Our commitment, then as now, was to the world of the Charter. . . In the service of this commitment . . . we dismantled the mightiest military force we had ever assembled. Armies were disbanded wholesale. . . Within two years after the end of the war, our defense spending had fallen by nearly $70 billion. Our armed forces were slashed. . . History has not seen, I believe, a more complete and comprehensive demonstration of a great nation's hope for peace and amity.

> US representative to the UN, Adlai Stevenson, speaking at the time of the Cuba Crisis in the General Assembly, 1962

(ii) Contrary to what is often believed in the West, the USSR made a very big reduction of its armed forces after the war, in fact reducing them to 25% of the 1945 figure, compared with the US reduction of 13%.

Considering that the USSR had long and potentially hostile frontiers in Europe, the Middle and the Far East, whereas the USA had atomic bombs and no potentially hostile frontiers bordering the USA itself, the 1948 total Soviet manpower figures of 2.9 million would hardly seem excessive from a purely military standpoint, when compared with the American 1.5 million.

> From P.M.S. Blackett, *Studies of War*, 1962

B The Dangers of Atomic Warfare

(i) At the time of the explosion [over Hiroshima], energy was given off in the forms of light, heat, radiation and pressure. The complete band of radiations, from X and gamma rays, through ultra-violet and light rays to the radiant heat of infra-red rays, travelled with the speed of light. The shock wave, created by the enormous pressure, built up almost instantaneously at the point of the explosion, but moved out more slowly, that is at about the speed of sound. . . The duration of the flash was only a fraction of a second, but it was sufficiently intense to cause third-degree burns to human skin up to a distance of a mile. . .

The blast wave which followed the flash was of sufficient force to press in the roofs of reinforced concrete structures and to flatten completely all less sturdy structures. Due to the height of the explosion, the peak pressure of the wave at ground zero was no higher than that produced by a near miss of a high explosive bomb and decreased at greater distances from ground zero. The blast wave, however, was of far greater extent and duration than that of a high explosive bomb and most reinforced concrete structures suffered structural damage or collapse up to 700ft at Hiroshima and 2000ft at Nagasaki. Brick buildings were flattened up to 7300ft at Hiroshima and 8500ft at Nagasaki.

From the *US Strategic Bombing Survey*, No. 4, 1947

(ii) There is a school of military thinking which . . . recognizes that when several nations have atomic bombs, a war which will destroy modern civilization will result and that no nation can win such a war. This school of thought therefore advocates a 'preventative war', an attack on Russia now before Russia has atomic bombs. If we should attempt to destroy all the principal Russian cities and her heavy industry, we might well succeed. But the immediate counter-measure which such an attack would call for is the prompt occupation of all continental Europe by the Red Army. Would we be prepared to destroy the cities of all Europe in trying to finish what we started? The idea is so contrary to all the basic instincts and principles of the American people that any such action would be possible only under a dictatorship at home.

Henry Wallace, in his *Letter to the President*, 1946

(iii) The pattern of the use of atomic weapons was set at Hiroshima. They are the weapons of aggression, of surprise and of terror. If they are ever used again, it may well be by thousands or by tens of thousands. . . But it is a weapon for aggressors and the elements of surprise and terror are as intrinsic to it as are the fissionable nuclei.

Dr J.R. Oppenheimer, quoted in *The Absolute Weapon*, 1947

C A Soviet Historian's Verdict on Khrushchev

Khrushchev was often called a public figure of the Lenin type – and indeed he had much in common with Lenin: candour, the resilience to withstand political setbacks, an oratorical style that fused polemic and popular appeal, the vigour and the courage to take risks, devotion to the Party. But he was also a disciple of Stalin and a product of the Stalin era, which had schooled him in political dexterity and left him a legacy of ruthlessness, discretion and the perspicacity to ignore certain obvious truths. In spite of these influences, Khrushchev was a highly original man with a great deal of natural talent, an unusually strong will and great buoyancy. He was remarkably independent – as many of his decisions indicate; unfortunately, however, he was always impatient, keen to pursue courses of action that, by their very nature, could not produce results as quickly as he anticipated. He often resorted to improvization – sometimes a useful political expedient but one that generally precipitated economic disaster. As a result he was often influenced by the unscrupulous and the venal and, having dismissed one corrupt official, frequently replaced him with another who was even worse.

Khrushchev did not escape the corrosive effects of absolute power and adulation. In the last years of his leadership his manner was increasingly that of a bully, and he became less and less self-critical, compounding his mistakes by refusing to acknowledge his failures. His withdrawal from politics was forced on him; yet even in the last hours of supremacy, as he parried the attacks of his opponents, power remained for him a means, not an end; he defended himself with words alone.

Khrushchev's record in power was chequered. He was certainly responsible for some notable errors of judgment. But he will be remembered for the achievements of those years – achievements that were largely inspired by him: the rehabilitation of millions of men and women who had suffered in Stalin's camps and prisons and in exile; the transformation of the system of collective farms as it had existed under Stalin; and the radical revision of the foreign policy of the Soviet Union. These and many other social and political reforms paved the way for further advances, which Khrushchev himself was unable to initiate. Few of them, alas, have been implemented by his successors – a sobering thought as we stand now on the threshold of a new era.

Roy Medvedev, *Khrushchev*, 1981

D Soviet Asian Policy After 1945

There are several good studies of a politico-economic nature on the Soviet Far East, but very few of Soviet policy *in* the Far East. Here the reactive myth has operated in reverse; until recently the view of a hyper-active Soviet diplomacy in post-war Asia was still widely held. According to the classic mythology, it was by means of Soviet directives, transmitted at the South-east Asia Youth Conference in February 1948 (the 'Calcutta Conference'), that the first wave of Asian revolution was stirred up. As Soviet expansionist aims were progressively thwarted in the West, by the Truman Doctrine, the Marshall Plan, the Berlin Airlift and the establishment of NATO, 'Moscow turned East'. While the victory of Chinese Communism was always hard to accommodate to the Machiavellian myth of the great Soviet conspiracy in Asia, the Korean War certainly fitted very nicely. As Malcolm Mackintosh has written in his textbook study of Soviet foreign policy:

'The year 1949 brought a strategic stalemate in Europe: no further Soviet territorial advance could be made... However, in the Far East an entirely new set of circumstances... opened up great possibilities for Soviet strategy. From 1949 to 1953 it was the Far East that claimed priority among planners of Soviet strategy in Moscow.'

Lately a rather more sceptical view has been taken of the Soviet commitment to revolution in Asia, which the current war in Indochina has revealed to be less than whole-hearted. By backward projection, a similar picture seems to obtain for the whole post-war period. Charles McLane's excellent study of Soviet strategies in South-east Asia under Lenin and Stalin demonstrates the low priority given to this area by the Russians after the war, and their poor level of knowledge and understanding of the area. The myth of the Calcutta Conference dies hard, but McLane has cut it severely down to size, as did Dr Ruth McVey previously in an important but neglected monograph. It is also doubtful whether David Dallin's unequivocal assertion that the Korean War was 'planned, prepared and initiated by Stalin' would be so widely accepted today, although this phase of Soviet policy still awaits closer study. The assumption that the Soviet Union still continued to call the shots during the war, to the extent of being able to influence the course of negotiations conducted by China and North Korea with the United States and its allies at Panmunjom, is also questionable.

John Gittings, *Touching the Tiger's Buttocks*, 1972

NB In Source D, the numerous footnotes have been omitted for the sake of brevity. These omissions do not alter the sense of the extract.

Questions

1 How do parts (i) and (ii) of Source A differ from each other? What do you consider is the explanation for these differences? **(4 marks)**

2 a) Which of the three parts of Source B in your view is likely to be the most objective? How far does the tone and content of the source you have selected bear out your choice? **(4 marks)**

   b) Explain the reasons for the differences between the remaining two sources. Show which, in your opinion, takes the less extreme view of the subject under discussion. **(4 marks)**

3 Do you consider Source C to provide a balanced assessment of Khrushchev? Use the source to justify your opinion. **(6 marks)**

4 In what ways (other than in subject-matter) does Source D differ from the other six Sources A, B and C? Do these make the source, in your view, more or less valuable than the others? **(6 marks)**

5 Select from seven Sources A–D the one which, in your view, is the most credible, and the one which is the least credible. Explain in both cases why and how you made your choice. **(6 marks)**

18 DEALING WITH EXAMINATION QUESTIONS

Specimen Source-based Question Answer

(See pages 5–9)

1 Using your own knowledge, explain the events directly leading to the signing of the Protocol from which Source A is taken. **(3 marks)**

Early in 1945 Soviet troops poured into eastern Germany. At a conference at Yalta in the Crimea in February the Allies agreed to the temporary division of Germany into zones, reparations for war damage and the ending of Nazism. In April Berlin was besieged and Hitler was trapped. Rather than face capture he committed suicide. Troops from East and West met on the river Spree. On 7 May Hitler's successor, Admiral Doenitz, signed an unconditional surrender to the Allies who then began the partition of the country. One of the early stages in this partition was another conference in August 1945 at Potsdam, which produced this Protocol (Source A).

2 Using Source B and your own knowledge, explain Winston Churchill's increasing dissatisfaction with the situation in eastern Europe in March 1946. **(3 marks)**

Though originally he had high hopes of post-war cooperation, Churchill became increasingly disillusioned with Soviet policies in eastern Europe and came to believe that they had 'expansive and proselytizing tendencies'. In his Fulton speech he listed the eastern European capitals that had been passed under Soviet rule, and asserted that an 'iron curtain' had 'descended across the continent'. Apart from Greece and Czechoslovakia he believed that these countries were now subject to 'control from Moscow' through the agency of small and unrepresentative communist parties. So strong was this feeling that shortly after the end of the war he instructed General Montgomery to keep the German armies intact in case they should have to be used against Russia.

3 With reference to Source C, explain the reasons why the United States concluded in September 1946 that the Soviet Union was violating the terms agreed in Source A. **(4 marks)**

The United States government did not believe that the Russians were willing to carry out the terms of the Potsdam agreement with regard to demilitarization and reparations. They believed that the Allied Control Council had failed 'to take the necessary steps to enable the German economy to function as an economic unit' and pointed out that a fair distribution of essential commodities between the zones had not been arranged, that the objective of achieving 'a balanced economy throughout Germany' had been frustrated and that zonal barriers were still a serious obstacle to German economic unity. Although he speaks of 'a military struggle for power between East and West', Byrnes stops short of naming the Soviet Union as being responsible for all infringements of terms 'expressly required by the Potsdam Agreement', but his implication is that it was Russian non-cooperation that had brought them about.

4 In what ways does the explanation given in Source D of Soviet policies in Europe, 1945–46, differ from those offered in Sources B and C?

(6 marks)

Source D ascribes Soviet policies in eastern Europe to an awareness of their own weaknesses rather than to any desire for expansion and conquest. Far from seeking to establish 'totalitarian control' through the creation of 'police states' the Russians are said to have pursued policies that are 'conservative and cautious'. Thus Source D explains Soviet actions more in terms of *realpolitik* than in terms of ideology. It admits that the Russians operated through small local parties, but does not agree with Churchill's opinion that they were all communists. Furthermore, Source D states that US and British forces had as little respect for unborn democracies as the Russians themselves, and instances Italy, Greece and Belgium as examples of their indifference. Anglo-British forces, like Russian ones, are said to have had no intention of allowing their strategic and economic interests to be endangered by local democracies. The source concludes by denying that the Russians ever had the intention of 'bolshevizing' eastern Europe. This flatly contradicts Source B, which places the blame squarely on the Soviet Union. It also differs in tone from Source C, which implies that the Soviet Union should bear all the odium of the 'military struggle for power between East and West'.

5 To what extent do Sources D and E offer more impartial explanations of Allied policies in post-war Europe than Sources B and C? What evidence of hindsight do Sources D and E contain? **(6 marks)**

Sources B and C take a partisan view of the East-West struggle in the immediate post-war years. Churchill is at his most eloquent in denouncing Soviet encroachment into Europe, and Byrnes likewise presents Russian failings with an air of certainty. Insofar as Source D distributes its criticisms more even-handedly, it may be said to be more impartial, though the reader may be pardoned for questioning whether Western interference in the establishment of new regimes in Italy or in Belgium was quite as blatant as communist interference in the new regimes in eastern Europe. Source E goes further in suggesting that there was little difference between the Eastern and the Western powers in their European policies; both, it is said, were dominated by selfish concerns, and neither regarded their 'mutual commitments' as anything more than a screen for their special interests. The source goes on to excuse any quarrels on the grounds that the agreements between the Allies were as vague as they were elaborate, with the result that differences were bound to occur.

Sources D and E both contain examples of hindsight. The assertion made in the last line of Source D, that 'the Russians had no intention of Bolshevizing Europe in 1945', clearly dates from the late 1960s, when Kolko's book was written; there were few who would have accepted this judgement in the late 1940s. In Source E, too, the assumption that both sides intended from the beginning to abandon their promises seems wise after the event; the 'divorce' which it regards as 'inevitable' in 1969 was inevitable only after it had happened.

6 Which of the five sources A–E in your opinion is the most reliable? How far do all the sources enable the historian to construct an accurate picture of events in Europe, 1945–46? **(8 marks)**

Sources D and E, written a number of years after the events which they describe, are typical secondary sources and are important for conveying the theories of the historians who are their authors. Sources A–C are more reliable in that they convey facts: in the case of Source B, the facts of Churchill's views on the 'iron curtain', and in the case of Source C the facts of Byrnes's views on the breakdown of occupation arrangements in Germany in 1946. Source A, however, seems the most reliable, since it is the English version (the other one being in Russian) of a protocol which the occupying powers agreed at Potsdam. No one would dispute the reliability of this text; nor could there be much dispute over its meaning.

As far as they go, these five sources cast light on the situation in post-war Europe from a number of different angles, three of them contemporary. The Western standpoint in Sources B and C is better represented than the Soviet one; but the later views help to redress the balance, and enable the reader to see the situation from both sides. However, whilst the sources give us a fairly rounded picture, and are consonant with the present state of historical knowledge, they are too few in number for us to conclude that their portrayal is totally accurate. Many more sources would have to be seen to accord with these five before we could presume we had a totally accurate picture, and even then it is always possible that documents may later come to light which would cause us to revise our views of these five.

Approaching Essay Questions

The key to writing successful essay answers, in the examination room or out of it, must always be *relevance* to the subject set. Relevance is worth much more than length or complexity of detail. Accurate knowledge is also important, but only if it is employed to back up a particular case, and not for its own sake. Pure narrative, even of an accurate kind, is less valuable than material directly focused on the subject of the question. Likewise prepared essays, even if well presented, will score very little if they do not bear directly on the subject set. Examiners are agreed that undue concentration on purely narrative or descriptive material, and regurgitation of prepared (but irrelevant) work are the two most common failings of examination answers. Conversely there is general agreement that the best answers are concise, analytical and always relevant. These answers also show signs of wide and careful reading, yet confine themselves to picking out a few key facts which best illustrate the theme of the answer. Finally they arrange and present the elements of the answer in the most effective way. This process, of course, is more difficult than it sounds: only constant practice will lead eventually to perfection.

Planning the essay

The planning of an examination essay must be done quickly, for most of the effort must go into writing the essay itself. In planning the scale of the work, you must have in mind the amount you are actually capable of writing in the time allowed, since this varies widely from one individual to another, according to the physical size and speed of your writing. Within these limits you must plan to make your treatment as comprehensive as possible.

First you should take the title and work out what it means and what areas it intends to probe. In every case, you should shape your preparatory material to suit the needs of the title, rather than loosening the focus of the title in order to include the material which you happen to have prepared.

Then the shape of the essay itself should be planned. Sometimes a few pencilled words – or even a diagrammatical plan – will suffice; or sometimes a more detailed synopsis may be needed. What is *not* needed is a lengthy plan which seriously detracts from the time available for the essay itself.

The shape of the essay

The essay should fall into three distinguishable parts:

1) **Introduction.** If you have thought out what you intend to say it should not be too difficult to summarize the argument that you are going to set out. The more punchy your introduction, the more it will engage the attention of the reader. The danger, unfortunately, is that students often seem obliged to resort to lengthy 'background' material which serves little purpose. They sometimes take refuge in the transparent stratagem of: 'Before answering this question it is necessary to answer another one.' It is better to have no introduction at all than one of this sort.

2) **The body of the essay.** This should develop your case fully. Each paragraph should make a particular point. Paragraphs should not be too long, and should be logically linked to the paragraph preceding. If you study a well-written essay you will find link words such as 'Moreover', 'Nevertheless' and 'However', or phrases such as 'On the other hand'. These are worked into the text to give it a logical structure. The idea behind the linkage is to lead the reader smoothly from one stage of the argument to the next in a sensible, orderly flow. However, it is unlikely that a complete essay will deal with nothing but argument; rather it will be composed of varying proportions of three ingredients:

a) **Narrative**, dealing with events in order from the earlier to the later. This is the familiar style in which many history textbooks are written.
b) **Description**, dealing with historical facts at a given moment in time, and relating to narrative as a still photograph does to a moving film.
c) **Analysis**, going further than description and explaining the relationships between the various aspects of the subject in a more rigorous way. The greater part of an essay at A-Level or Higher Grade should be at this level of abstraction, rather than at the lower levels of narrative and description. The recipe recommended by Professor G.R. Elton is one of 'Narrative thickened by analysis'.

3) **The conclusion.** This should draw together the threads of the argument and bring it to a logical end. Obviously, the more conclusive the argument of the essay, the fewer loose ends and unanswered questions will be left. Unfortunately in practice many conclusions turn out to be no more than a tiresome repetition of what has just been written, and thus lack the force that they should have. It is better to have no conclusion at all than one of this sort.

Types of essay

What most essays call for is analysis, comparison or evaluation. Of course, there may be elements of description in the way the essay is presented, or narrative links which help to carry the essay forward; but what you are usually asked for at A-Level or Higher Grade is *argument*, and what examiners value most highly is the ability to argue a case. Too often candidates put themselves on the familiar tramlines of some piece of narrative that they have memorized, and are happy to follow them without realizing that they are heading in the wrong direction. This temptation may become irresistible in the heat of an examination, but its results are often disastrous.

There is almost an infinite variety in the sort of history titles which may be set, but it remains a fact that most of them may be said to be one of four types:

1) **List questions** are of a descriptive and analytical type: here you are asked to list factors of one sort or another – causes, results, or features. You

may be asked to 'explain' why there was an international crisis over Berlin in 1948, or what were the 'effects' or 'consequences' on international relations of the Cuban Missiles crisis in 1962. Or you may be asked to 'describe' United States involvement in Latin America in its struggle against communism in the 1970s and 1980s, and have to pick out and discuss examples of such involvement in a variety of different countries. List questions may ask directly for the evidence supporting or refuting a particular viewpoint, as for example: '"The late sixties may have seen the start of a new development in history: the era of conflict between states perhaps giving way to a period of conflict within states, between government and governed." What evidence supports this view?' In such a case, the evidence selected has to be set out.

2) **Yes/No questions** invite affirmation or denial, asking you to consider and comment on a particular judgement offered. It may be suggested to you that 'The Soviet invasion of Afghanistan in 1979 was Brezhnev's greatest blunder', and you may be asked to 'discuss', 'comment on' or 'consider' this verdict. You may even be asked 'Do you agree?' At their simplest, such questions may be answered in a single word, 'Yes' or 'No', though answers of such brevity are not recommended. What you are being invited to do is to review the arguments on both sides of the question. You do not have to feel that as an impartial observer you have to sit on the fence; in practice the examiner will not penalize you for having a view, provided that you have argued it through and given a fair hearing to both sides.

3) **'How far?' questions** ask you to consider the relative significance of a given person or event in a particular historical situation. You may be asked 'how far' or 'to what extent' did Khrushchev's advocacy in 1956 of peaceful co-existence lead in the next ten years to a genuine improvement in East-West relations; or you may be presented with a quotation such as 'The creation of a Russian satellite empire in eastern Europe after 1945 was, seen from Moscow, merely a sensible defensive strategy but to the Western powers it had all the appearance of aggressive imperialism', and be asked 'to what extent' this was true. All such questions demand analysis, evaluation and historical judgement of one kind or another.

4) **Comparison questions** ask you to 'compare' Stalin and Khrushchev as Cold War leaders, or to 'contrast' Soviet reactions to the Hungarian rising of 1956 and the Czech rising of 1968. Or, simultaneously, to 'compare and contrast'. In fact there is not a lot of difference. The first, literally, means to 'find the similarities' and the second to 'find the differences'; but in practice it is difficult to do one without doing the other. A comparison question may present you with a choice, such as: 'Which presented a greater danger to world peace, the Berlin crisis of 1948–49 or the Cuban Missiles crisis of 1962?' Though this seems a one-phrase-answer question, closer examination shows it to be a comparison of the two crises.

Final Note

In tackling most history questions a variety of different approaches are perfectly possible. For this reason, 'model' answers should be treated with some caution. Most examiners will admit not only that some of the best work they have seen is short and pithy, but the best essays sometimes plot an unexpected course to an answer. Answers which contain an element of surprise start off with the distinct advantage of engaging the interest of the examiner; if they sustain this advantage through their own merits the candidate is well on the road to success.

There are books available which deal in some depth with issues connected with question analysis and essay preparation. Students may well find some of the following useful:

C. Brasher: *The Young Historian* (OUP, 1970)
J. Cloake, V. Crinnon & S. Harrison: *The Modern History Manual* (Framework Press, 1987)
J. Fines: *Studying to Succeed – History at A-Level and Beyond* (Longman, 1986)
D.M. Sturley: *The Study of History* (Longmans Green, 1969)

The following list of essay titles on the Cold War includes suggestions – no more than suggestions! – on how to approach them, plus a specimen answer for one of them. Use them as part of your course or for examination practice.

Possible Essay Titles

The essay titles listed below are taken from A-Level questions in Paper 269/1, as set by the University of London Examinations and Assessment Council, and are reproduced by their kind permission*.

1 Why, and when, did it become clear that four-power occupation in Germany would lead to the lasting two-part division of the country? (*Type 1*)

This is a two-part question, and roughly equal weight will be given in the marking to 'Why?' and 'When?'. Care should be taken in the first part to produce an *explanation* and not merely a narrative; the question asks 'Why?' and not 'How?'. In answering the first part, evidence must be brought of the deep differences developing between the Soviet Union and the Western powers: differences over administration leading to a deadlock in the Council of Foreign Ministers, inability to agree terms for future

* *Disclaimer:* The University of London School Examinations Board accepts no responsibility whatsoever for the accuracy or method of working in the answers given.

unification, quarrels relating to policies regarding reparations, displaced persons, forced labour and reconstruction. Marshall Aid and proposed currency reform led to the Berlin Blockade and resulted in the new defensive military alignments in 1949 and 1955. At the same time it should be shown that the differences between the Western powers were less intractable: the USA and Britain did not find it hard to merge their zones at the end of 1946, and France came into the merger later. The second part ('*When?*') requires you to make a judgement on how soon it was before the division of Germany appeared likely to be lasting. More perceptive commentators reached this conclusion fairly early with the decline of goodwill after the breakdown of the London talks at the end of 1945. It became increasingly obvious later, and there could be no denying it by the time the Berlin Blockade began in June 1948. Subsequent developments merely confirmed a pattern that had already been laid down.

2 'More justification existed for the Marshall Plan than for the Truman Doctrine.' How far do you agree? (*Type 4*)

This is the sort of question requiring a *comparison* between two subjects, and not merely two consecutive statements placed end-to-end so that the examiner has the materials to make his own comparison. In commenting on the quotation, you are not obliged either to accept what it says, or reject it; but it is desirable that you should do one or the other, and that your decision should be adequately supported by arguments. The justification which underlay the Marshall Plan was of the widest nature, and arose from the post-war economic condition of Europe, which it is proper to comment on at some length; it aimed at reconstruction, and the urgency of this could not be denied at the time. Insofar as the Plan was sincere in its assertion that it was not 'directed against any country or doctrine', its aid was available to eastern as well as western Europe and was not primarily a political or diplomatic weapon. If not actually disinterested, it was certainly humanitarian. The Truman Doctrine, however, was specifically conceived as a check to what was seen in Washington as a communist threat in the Balkan area, and later elsewhere; and substantial dollar aid 'to assist free peoples to work out their own destinies in their own way' was one main way of checking this threat. But perhaps you may be tempted to develop the argument that the same underlying motives prompted both policies, these being dominated by power politics and commercial exploitation; so that in neither case were US objectives as disinterested as they pretended to be.

3 Why was Berlin partitioned in 1945, blockaded in 1948, and divided by the Wall in 1961? (*Type 1*)

This is a three-part question, each part asking '*Why?*'. Description of each event should therefore be kept to a minimum, and the bulk of the answer should concentrate on reasons. Your answer should show good understanding of the circumstances of 1945 in which it seemed desirable that the responsibility for Berlin should be shared amongst the victorious allies; the problems of German reconstruction and the increasing distrust between East and West at the time of the Marshall Plan which led to Stalin's attempt to besiege the city; and the problems of East German emigration and the efforts of the East German Government to secure recognition from the West which led to the building of the Wall in 1961.

4 'A purely defensive alliance': can this description be applied equally to the North Atlantic Treaty Organization of 1949 and the Warsaw Pact of 1955? (*Type 4*)

This question is again a *comparison* question, requiring you to examine the purposes for which NATO and the Warsaw Pact were established, and to decide whether or not they were both defensive alliances. Intelligent reference should be made to the circumstances leading to the conclusion of both alliances, and the terms of the two treaties (particularly the two preambles to the treaties) may be used to show how closely the second treaty mirrored the first. The title provides you with an opportunity to explode the myth that the purposes of the NATO treaty were purely defensive, and brought about by Stalin's unreasonable behaviour over the Berlin blockade, whilst the Warsaw Pact was part of an aggressive communist strategy to subvert and take over the West. At the same time, the greater freedom of the Western powers in their relationship to their alliance should be contrasted with the monolithic structure of the Warsaw Pact in practice under Soviet leadership.

5 How valid is it to see the ideological divide between the US and the USSR in the twenty years after the end of the Second World War as being a smokescreen for their national fears and rivalries rather than the real source of conflict between the two powers? (*Type 3*)

This question is one of the more difficult *'How far?'* questions, involving a judgement of the relative validity of two quite different approaches to the subject. In a sense it is an unanswerable question, since in the last analysis the answer is a matter of opinion – and an opinion over which historians much better qualified than you (or me!) are still arguing. The subject provides a contrast between the *Hegelian* interpretation, which argues that ideology is the mainspring which determines the facts of political and economic conflict, and the *Marxist* interpretation, which argues conversely that economic fears and rivalries are the mainspring and determine the appropriate ideologies. On the one hand there is no doubt that there were severely practical considerations which drove the Soviet Union into perpetuating its control over much of eastern Europe, and deep-seated material interests of a diplomatic, strategical and economic sort which underlay the thinking which led to the Marshall Plan and the Truman Doctrine; but on the other the philosophic justification of both American and Russian leaders arose from genuine conviction in the rightness of their democratic and the communist causes. To diminish the force of these striving ideologies by calling them a 'smokescreen' prejudges the question, and betrays the fundamental assumptions of the questioner.

6 Account for the involvement of the USA in the Korean War. To what extent had the United States government achieved its objectives in Korea by the end of 1953? (*Type 1/3*)

The answer falls into two parts, and approximately equal weight will be given by the examiner to each part. In the first part, the domestic as well as the international circumstances of the USA in 1950 should be explained, as both have a clear bearing on the answer. You should acknowledge the strength of the US initiative in a situation which enabled it to jockey the UN into the struggle. To answer the question in the second sentence, of course, it is necessary to have decided what the objectives of the USA were before you can judge whether they were achieved or not. The US government brought the conflict successfully to an end, but the solution was never any better than a rather messy compromise, and one achieved at very considerable cost. As a strategy for checking the forces of communism in China or the Far East generally, or for stamping America's moral authority on the treatment of world disputes, it was obviously a non-starter.

7 What threats was the involvement of the USA in Korea and Indochina designed to resist? (*Type 1*)

This is a *list* question in which a paragraph should be written about each of the threats you identify to the USA in these two regions. Commercial, military, political and ideological threats should be explained and described. There should be some indication whether the United States was acting (in your opinion) purely on its own behalf, or whether its interests genuinely represented the interests of the 'free world'. The question may be taken to imply that the threats were the same in both cases; if you do not accept this, you have to explain how they were different. For instance, whilst it might be argued that the Korean intervention was designed against any effort to weaken the authority of the United Nations, this could not be said for Vietnam, since the Organization was not involved. Hence there is an element of *comparison* between Korea and Vietnam implicit in the question, though this should not be made into a major feature of your answer.

8 What international crises occurred in 1956 in Europe and the Middle East, and how did the USA and the USSR respond to them? (*Type 1*)

This question may seem rather easier than others, since at the beginning it contains a strong descriptive element of the Hungarian and Suez crises. In each case, however, the description of the crises must be followed by an explanation of the Soviet and US responses to the crises. Whilst this in itself is also partly descriptive, it has to be reasoned through. Were the two

powers consistent in their responses to them? Were the responses
statesmanlike and far-sighted, or did one or other of the powers seek to use
the crises to maximize their own advantages and realize their own national
objectives? Answers will probably fall into two parts, dealing with crises and
responses in each case; the best will make clear not only *how* but *why* the
responses of the two powers were different. Britain, France and Israel may
feature in the course of the answer but are not the main focus of it.

9 To what extent did Khrushchev's advocacy in 1956 of 'peaceful
co-existence' lead during the next ten years to genuine improvements
in East-West relations? *(Type 3)*

A descriptive review is required here of international developments in the
decade 1956–66, in each case measuring up the episode described to see
whether it fits the criterion of 'peaceful co-existence'. The U2 crisis, the
quarrels at the Paris summit in 1960, the resurgence of the Berlin question
and the building of the Wall in 1961 seem to be disappointing auguries for
co-existence, and the high tension of the Cuba crisis in 1962 to an even
greater degree showed the dangers underlying US-Soviet relations. The
resolution of the Cuba crisis, however, the signature of the Test-Ban
Treaty and the installation of the 'Hot Line' did go some way towards
renewing *détente*. Answers should also feature the fact that China's refusal
to accept the philosophy of peaceful co-existence, their criticism of the
change in Soviet policies, and their own adventurism in Ladakh and
elsewhere made an overall *détente* in East-West relations impossible.

10 'Stalin after 1945 and Khrushchev pursued similar objectives in foreign
policy; only their methods were different.' Examine the truth of this
statement. *(Type 2/4)*

This question calls for a comparison between the foreign policy methods
and objectives of two Soviet leaders, and to this extent is a type 4 question;
but it requires also a judgement, which may be of the 'Yes/No' (type 2)
variety or may be of the 'To some extent' (type 3) kind. What is *not* wanted
is a lengthy factual description of the post-war foreign policies of Stalin,
end-to-end with factual descriptions of Khrushchev's foreign policies: this
merely provides the raw material for an answer. It could be argued that the
fundamental objectives of all foreign policies (if they are good policies)
should be the same, in that they involve the best defence in the
circumstances of the country's interests; but this is not the full story. Stalin,
for instance, like his former colleague Trotsky, held firmly to the inherent
superiority of the communist system and thus imparted a certain
missionary zeal to his foreign policies; whereas Khrushchev, seeking for
'co-existence' with the West either out of weakness or out of lack of
conviction, made the damaging admission that his enemy's ideas were as
good as his own. This means that Khrushchev followed much more closely
ideas of *realpolitik* than did Stalin, though even Khrushchev continued to

use the same communist rhetoric e.g. over Cuba. On the other hand, the methods of Stalin and Khrushchev, dictated by an inner knowledge of their own weaknesses, both consisted of bluff, propaganda and a rigid insistence on the importance of 'solidarity' to their cause, and they backed them up with military and technological might and the apparatus of totalitarian control. One might even be inclined to think that it was the methods of the foreign policies of the two leaders that were the same, and the objectives that were different.

11 What issues were at stake in the Cuban Missiles Crisis? How true is it that the crisis ended a period of frantic competition for nuclear supremacy between the USA and the Soviet Union? (*Type 1/3*)

The phrase 'what issues' in the first sentence makes this question a *list* question, and examiners will allow about half the available credit for this part of the answer. The other sentence calls for a *judgement* of how far the Cuba crisis moved international relations in the direction of *détente*. In the short run they obviously did, but the fall of Khrushchev in 1964, the reimposition of hard-line thinking in the Kremlin under Brezhnev and the explosion of a nuclear device at Lop Nor by the Chinese in the same year meant that the pause in the struggle was never any better than short-lived.

12 'It was a great victory for us . . . that we had been able to extract from Kennedy a promise that neither America nor any of her allies would invade Cuba.' (*Khrushchev Remembers*) How far do you agree with Khrushchev's verdict on the Missiles Crisis, 1962? (*Type 3*)

This is an analytical question that hinges round a quotation – not an uncommon format for a question at this level. You are being asked to decide whether the Cuban crisis is to be seen merely as a successful Soviet effort to avert a US invasion of Cuba, or whether it ranged over much bigger and wider issues. There can be little doubt that it did. Some of these issues were of domestic concern for the United States, touching the exposed nerve of American fears about communism in the western hemisphere; others reached much further afield – though perhaps Khrushchev, who did not emerge from the crisis very strongly, is to be forgiven for playing its importance down. This is an opportunity to display your grasp of the world roles of the two major participants – the Soviet Union and the USA.

13 Explain the theory and assess the practice of peaceful co-existence in United States-Soviet relations in the period 1956–74. (*Type 1*)

This is perhaps an easier question that it seems at first sight. The explanation of the *theory* of peaceful co-existence may not go quite so far as to merit half the available marks, but if not the balance of the marks will be on offer for the *assessment* in the second part. The theory should be stated as simply as possible, and should focus on the advantages which prompted peaceful co-existence. In the second part there should be a contrast between theory and practice, showing how, within the date-limits laid down, the achievements of peaceful co-existence, though often quite substantial, foundered on the ultimately intransigent attitudes of both the USSR and USA. Some treatment of key episodes such as the Czechoslovak Spring of 1968 will give substance to the answer.

14 'Improved relations with the USA, but embittered relations with China': how adequately do these phrases summarize the results of Khrushchev's foreign policy? (*Type 3*)

There are two aspects to this question, and they ought to be given approximately equal treatment. In the first part, some of the material used in Question 9 could be usefully employed, though it should be noted that the question is confined to Khrushchev's period of office and should not be stretched much beyond 1964. In the second part there is space for a brief consideration of the factors leading to the Sino-Soviet dispute, but the important thing is to examine the results of the quarrel and to show not only how the ideological quarrel between them led to embitterment, but how more practical matters, such as the war on the Far Eastern frontier and the suspension of industrial and financial support for Mao, led to deep mutual resentment which Brezhnev struggled in vain to moderate.

15 'A new Cold War: Moscow v Peking.' Discuss Sino-Soviet relations, 1960–80, in the light of this description of them. (*Type 3*)

This is a straightforward application of a quoted assessment to a given historical situation. This time the causes of the Sino-Soviet dispute must be described in detail, since an explanation of how this Cold War between them came into being is a vital part of the answer. Their mutual grievances may be provided in the form of an elaborated list. In the second part there should be proper chronological coverage of the interval specified, identifying and describing the main episodes which give evidence of this Cold War. The answer should end with the Soviet invasion of Afghanistan, explaining the reasons for Chinese resentment of Soviet actions in that country.

16 How far can it be argued that a Cold War between the United States and the Soviet Union has continued to exist since 1970? (*Type 3*)

The question seeks to probe the effectiveness of the *détente* process since 1970, and thus demands an analytical balancing of the successes of *détente* against its failures. In some episodes, such as the Soviet invasion of Afghanistan, Cold War temperatures fell very low; but on other occasions, as at the CSCE Conference at Helsinki in 1975, a little warmth crept into the relationship. The passing of the Old Guard in the Kremlin in 1985 with the accession to office of Gorbachev, with consequent encouraging signs at Reykjavik in 1986, and the replacement of the hard-line Reagan by the more malleable Bush as Republican President of the US in 1989 began a vigorous effort to thaw out the Cold War. Events in 1991 seemed to carry these to their logical conclusion.

17 Why did the involvement of the USA in Indochina after 1954 excite such widespread condemnation? (*Type 1*)

The condemnation of US involvement in Indochina by the communist bloc needs to be explained, though perhaps it was never unexpected. Nor were the attitudes of the USSR and Communist China the same: their differences should be carefully charted and accounted for. Where the question goes somewhat beyond the Cold War (and you have no right to expect your examiners to confine themselves religiously to what you see as one of the key topics in the syllabus!) is that US actions in Indochina were also criticized, and sometimes condemned, by powers which previously had been numbered amongst the USA's allies. Australia participated in the Vietnam War with increasing ill-grace, but other powers such as Britain, normally very staunch in its support of the USA, questioned the need for it. It is perhaps the criticism of America's friends rather than the hostility of its rivals which needs to be examined.

18 To what extent did the Conference on Security and Co-operation in Europe at Helsinki in 1975 consolidate the movement towards East-West *détente*? (*Type 3*)

See the specimen answer on pages 119–21.

19 How do you explain the involvement of the Soviet Union in Afghanistan in the years 1978–88, and to what extent has that involvement been misrepresented by hostile propaganda? (*Type 3*)

The answer to this question falls into two parts. In the first part, Soviet involvement is more easily described than explained, though it is explanation that the question asks for. The Soviet leadership saw itself ensnared in the country in much the same way that the United States had been ensnared in Vietnam, driven to the invasion by considerations relating to internal stability and external security, rather than by ideological factors. It was only the USSR's rivals who took a less charitable view, regarding it as another example of Soviet expansionism. In this matter, China's objections to the Soviet action were much the same as those originating in the West: the Afghan regime Brezhnev supported was little more than a puppet regime used to furnish the excuse for an unmerited aggression; the Soviet Union was showing its usual scant regard for the rights of its neighbours; the Brezhnev Doctrine was being quite unjustifiably stretched to cover the absorption of more territory into the Soviet Empire, and so on. These, however, were the unsympathetic reactions of hostile outsiders. It is your task, in writing a balanced assessment, to consider what factors really drove the Kremlin into incurring such international opprobrium.

20 For what reasons, and with what success, have the super-powers attempted to put a brake on the arms race since 1962? (*Type 1/3*)

In tackling such an area as disarmament under the topic of the Cold War, it is desirable that you should have familiarized yourself with a list of the initiatives towards disarmament that have been taken after 1945. The question covers all types of disarmament, both nuclear and conventional, though a concentration on the nuclear aspect will give you quite enough to do. It is not necessary, however, for you to go through your list item by item, but merely to reveal your grasp of the facts as far as they can be employed in constructing a relevant answer. You should distinguish between arms control and disarmament. What is wanted here is a statement of *reasons* (Type 1 essay) and an assessment of *success* (Type 3 essay). Again the two halves of the question may not be exactly equal; but what credit you do not gain in the first part will normally be made available for the second. The first part may be dealt with in fairly general terms, and will hinge largely on the immense destructiveness of modern war, and on the relatively attractive alternative of devoting the enormous resources involved to more peaceful developments. The second part, however, should be given more chronological treatment by examining the various initiatives and accounting for the various failures. Domestic factors relating to the situation within the negotiating countries as well as international factors are relevant here.

Specimen Essay Answer

(See page 118)

The answer below is not a model answer, nor does it represent the only approach. Nevertheless, it is an answer which focuses on the question and which represents the type of answer which may be written under examination conditions, in about 45 minutes.

To what extent did the Conference on Security and Co-operation in Europe at Helsinki in 1975 consolidate the movement towards East-West *détente*?

There were convincing signs of *détente* well before 1975. Early in Nixon's Presidency delegations from the USA and the USSR began the talks in Helsinki which led to the conclusion of SALT 1. In 1970 the Non-proliferation Treaty agreed in 1968 was ratified. In 1971 the powers signed the Sea-bed Treaty, banning the siting of nuclear weapons on the floor of the oceans, and agreed to the Quadripartite Agreement on Berlin, long regarded as the major sticking-point in satisfactory East-West relations in Germany. Also in 1971 there was an agreement to improve the 'hot-line' links between Washington and Moscow, and another to avoid nuclear war resulting from the accidental or unauthorized launching of nuclear weapons. In 1972 Nixon was given a warm welcome on his visit to Moscow, and these agreements went further. The SALT 1 Treaty was signed, substantially restricting the numbers of ICBMs and SLBMs, and this was followed by commercial treaties in the summer permitting large sales of American grain to the Soviet Union. There was also an agreement in 1973 on the 'Prevention of Nuclear War', which some regarded at the time as marking the end of the Cold War.

Nixon visited the USSR a second time in 1974. Further treaties resulted. One banned nuclear weapons tests underground if they yielded explosions greater than 150 kilotons; another amended their earlier agreement by limiting their ICBMs even more strictly in an Interim Agreement on Strategic Weapons. The two leaders also set in motion the long process of negotiation in a Conference on Security and Co-operation in Europe which eventually produced the Helsinki Agreement in August 1975, whose Final Act was signed by 35 interested states.

The Agreement was one of the most comprehensive steps ever taken in the direction of East-West *détente*. It fell into four grouped sections, or 'baskets' as they were known. The first related to security in Europe, and covered topics like sovereignty, peaceful settlement of disputes, human rights, self-determination, peaceful co-operation and disarmament. In particular, a number of its clauses, such as those concerning the inviolability of frontiers and the territorial integrity of states, helped towards a solution of the question of the two Germanies. 'Basket' Two dealt with co-operation in the field of economics, of science and technology and of the environment, dealing in detail with trade and industrial co-operation and the social problems arising out of migrant labour. The third 'basket' dealt with humanitarian matters relating to tourism, travel, the family and youth, and promised co-operation in the field of information, and the fourth set out the future steps by which the powers intended to follow up the conference.

Partly as a result of this agreement hopes ran high in the middle 1970s that the move towards East-West *détente* would soon be consolidated. President Carter, who was elected to power in the USA after the brief interregnum of Gerald Ford, was well-known to have a lively interest in human rights, and was likely to want this part of the agreement to work and to do his best to see that Brezhnev also implemented its provisions. The leaders of the two German states had a direct interest in resolving a dispute that had bedevilled East-West relations for more than a generation, and were both clearly anxious to use the Helsinki provisions to strengthen their own tenure of power in the Federal Republic and the Democratic Republic. All the major powers had an interest in the limitations proposed for future military manoeuvres and in disarmament proposals, especially nuclear disarmament.

Unfortunately these high hopes in a number of cases fell short of realization. This was partly because the Helsinki Agreement often stopped short of recommending solutions and confined itself to identifying and listing problems needing solution. Partly too, as in the case of human rights, it was couched in very general terms, and the Carter interpretation of what human rights should be was likely to be vastly different from the Brezhnev interpretation. Besides, as an International Commission of Jurists pointed out in 1978, the same 'basket' which guaranteed human rights also contained clauses on 'non-interference in the internal affairs of states' which in practice went a good way towards negating them. Hardly surprisingly, therefore, little of practical value was accomplished.

In the case of Germany, too, the Helsinki Agreement fell far short of being a peace settlement. What it did, however, was to provide a perfect opportunity for East Germany in particular to champion the continental status quo, and of course its place in it. Thus, Honecker singled out those aspects of the agreement which were the most important to him – the inviolability of frontiers, the sovereign equality of states and the principle of non-interference in the the affairs of other states – and transformed these 'security-related' features into a guarantee for the future existence of the Democratic Republic, insisting that they were preconditions for future East-West co-operation. As time passed, these efforts were seen less as a search for a solution for the German question than as a desperate effort to keep the East German communist regime in being.

The pursuit of disarmament also proved to be illusory. Carter grew steadily more disillusioned with what he saw as Brezhnev's bad faith over human rights, and with the Soviet invasion of Afghanistan in 1979 the hope of reconciliation vanished altogether. The invasion brought an immediate reaction. The NATO powers decided to instal new medium-range nuclear missiles in Europe, and the latest products of US technology in the form of Cruise and Pershing missiles began to replace the old weaponry. When Reagan was elected President in 1980 a new hard-line right-wing government took over in Washington. The recently-agreed SALT 2 agreement failed to be ratified and the US government began to increase rather than to cut military spending. Trade sanctions were imposed on the Soviet government. Hence the outlook at the start of the 1980s seemed much gloomier than it had been five years earlier.

Any consolidation of the move towards East-West *détente* as the result of the Helsinki Conference therefore proved to be short-lived. The industrial-military complex dominating US policy from the Pentagon was more powerful under Reagan than ever before, its attitudes increasingly more uncompromising; whilst the old-guard conservatives in the Kremlin, given their head by Brezhnev in his later years and by his two immediate successors, were also determined not to seem to give way to American pressure. The era of change was in fact close at hand, but nobody at the time could have foreseen it.

BIBLIOGRAPHY

This bibliography is not exhaustive. The basic books are marked with no asterisks, and are generally available, often in paperback. Books marked with one asterisk (*) include those which may be in use as textbooks at A-Level, not all of whose chapters are on this subject. Those marked with two asterisks (**) are less readily available, but may still be found in libraries by teachers and students.

Stephen E. Ambrose: *Rise to Globalism* (Allen Lane, 1972. Fifth revised edition, 1988). A useful and readable short account, though it covers the topic mainly from the American angle.

R.D. Cornwell: *World History in the Twentieth Century* (Longman, new edition, 1984), Part 3. A simple introduction at a fairly elementary level, useful for those just beginning the subject. The new edition is disappointing in that it misses the opportunity to update and revise the judgements made in the original.

D.F. Fleming: *The Cold War and Its Origins* (Doubleday & Co., NY, 1961). In two volumes, but finishes around 1960. Immensely detailed and impressive, though written from the American angle (it refers to Western policies as 'our' policies). Excellent quotations and references. Other books often owe more to this presentation than they acknowledge.

Louis J. Halle: *The Cold War as History* (Chatto & Windus, 1967). Knowledgeable and well-expressed, but sometimes rather slanted towards the West. Stops shortly after the Cuban Crisis.

Hugh Higgins: *The Cold War* (Heinemann Educational, Studies in Modern History, second edition, 1984). A first-class summary, short, but readable and informative. Excellent references and bibliography, though some of the books mentioned are not readily available to the ordinary student.

David Horowitz: *The Free World Colossus* (MacGibbon & Kee, 1965). Short, but well-written and instructive. Questions established interpretations, and often gives a refreshing new perspective. But still primarily a study of American foreign policy in the years to 1965.

Paul Johnson: *A History of the Modern World: from 1917 to the 1980s* (Wiedenfield & Nicholson, 1984 PB). Chapters 12–20. Slanted, but thought-provoking and always worth reading; parts of it do not relate to this topic.

George F. Kennan: *Russia and the West* (Mentor, New American Library, 1961 PB). Chapters 21–25. Authoritatively written by a former US diplomat, but relevant only in its final chapters. Terminates in 1960.

A.B. Lancaster: *From Containment to Co-existence: Foreign Policy of the United States, 1945–73* (Edward Arnold, Archive Series, Hill & Fell, 1975 PB). Handy collection of documents, but all from the US angle. Little editorial commentary.

Martin Macauley: *The Origins of the Cold War* (Longman, Seminar Studies in History, Third Impression, 1986). Good short account, with useful documents. Excellent bibliography, though some of the books mentioned are not readily available to the ordinary student.

Roger Morgan: *The Unsettled Peace: A Study of the Cold War in Europe* (BBC Publications, 1974). Good short account, with useful date-list and documents. But stops in 1973, and material limited to Europe.

E.G. Rayner: *International Affairs* (Edward Arnold, History of the Twentieth Century, Corebook, 1984). Elementary account, useful for those who are just beginning the topic.

**Adam B. Ulam: *Expansion and Co-existence* (Secker & Warburg, 1968). Very persuasively put, but a far from impartial account.

*Jack Watson: *World History Since 1945* (John Murray, 1989). Edited by Brendan O'Leary, after the author's death. Solid, workmanlike and impeccably accurate account, chiefly aimed at London Board candidates. Well-indexed, directing students to relevant chapters.

**W.A. Williams: *The Tragedy of American Diplomacy* (A Delta book, Dell Publishing, NY, 1972). Chiefly Chapters 6–8. Tightly argued, and not always easy to cope with, but contains some useful ideas.

INDEX